TWAYNE'S ENGLISH AUTHORS SERIES

Thomas Percy

TEAS 313

Thomas Percy

THOMAS PERCY

By BERTRAM H. DAVIS

Florida State University

TWAYNE PUBLISHERS

A DIVISION OF G. K. HALL & CO., BOSTON

Copyright © 1981 by G. K. Hall & Co.

Published in 1981 by Twayne Publishers,
A Division of G. K. Hall & Co.
All Rights Reserved

Printed on permanent/durable acid-free paper and bound
in the United States of America

First Printing

Frontispiece : mezzotint by W. Dickinson, 1775,
from oil painting by Sir Joshua Reynolds

Library of Congress Cataloging in Publication Data

Davis, Bertram Hylton.
Thomas Percy.

(Twayne's English authors series ; TEAS 313)
Bibliography: p. 158–66
Includes index.
1. Percy, Thomas, Bp. of Dromore, 1729–1811.
2. Literary historians—England—Biography.
PR29.P4D38   821'.044'09 [B]   80–23975
ISBN 0–8057–6804–1

For Ruth

Contents

About the Author

After ten years of teaching, first at Hunter and later at Dickinson College, Bertram H. Davis joined the staff of the American Association of University Professors and became, successively, editor of the *AAUP Bulletin*, deputy general secretary, and general secretary. In 1974 he joined the faculty of Florida State University, where he is now professor of English. His primary scholarly interest has been the Johnson circle, and he is the author of *Johnson before Boswell* and *A Proof of Eminence: The Life of Sir John Hawkins*, and the editor of an abridged edition of Hawkins's *Life of Johnson*. Professor Davis has all three degrees from Columbia University, plus an LL.D. from Dickinson College, and he was a Guggenheim Fellow in 1974. He is one of Twayne's field editors for the English Authors Series.

Preface

A scholar seeking to justify a life devoted to scholarship could do no better than to look to the late eighteenth century, and particularly to the Johnson circle. In 1776 Sir John Hawkins and Charles Burney published the rival histories of music that have influenced musicologists ever since. The years between 1774 and 1788 saw the appearance of Thomas Warton's *History of English Poetry*, the first attempt at a comprehensive study, and Edward Gibbon's *Decline and Fall of the Roman Empire*, perhaps the best known of all modern histories. Johnson himself—critic, essayist, journalist, poet—completed his *Dictionary of the English Language* in 1755 after almost nine years' labor; and he followed it in 1765 with his edition of Shakespeare, which, with the impetus later given to it by George Steevens and Edmond Malone, was to lead to the first of the variorum editions.

Scholarship, in short, attracted many of the best minds of the period, and scholars like Hawkins, Burney, Warton, and Malone have been remembered along with the poets and novelists who were their contemporaries. And even Johnson is no less celebrated for the "harmless drudgery" of his scholarly work than for his novel, his poems, and his essays: the very notes of his Shakespeare edition have been twice reprinted in recent decades. The lesson for any aspiring or dejected scholar is clear. Scholarship supported by imagination, industry, and taste can create works of the first rank and leave a lasting mark on a nation's character and letters.

Not the least among the Johnson circle's scholars was Thomas Percy, who came into the world a grocer's son and left it an Anglican bishop, but rose to fame on a collection of poems that captured the imaginations not just of his contemporaries but of generations of readers. The 1765 *Reliques of Ancient English Poetry*—Percy's *Reliques*, as it came to be known—was only one of numerous scholarly enterprises undertaken by Percy during his early years as a clergyman in rural Northamptonshire, but it is the primary reason for his being remembered, as well as for this study.

Much has been written about the *Reliques* in the more than two centuries since its first publication, and the present study can make little claim to originality in its central chapter about that work. Indeed, its indebtedness to scholars like Albert B. Friedman and the editors of *The Percy Letters* goes far beyond the occasional citations in the text or acknowledgments in the notes. What the study attempts for the first time is to see the *Reliques* in the full context of Percy's long scholarly career: to survey almost the entire body of his work, which was extensive and significant, although understandably just about everything else that he wrote has been overshadowed if not totally obscured by the *Reliques*.

In preparing this study I have had much assistance, which I am pleased to have an opportunity to acknowledge. To the late James L. Clifford I am indebted for constant encouragement and general advice, as well as for suggestions on particular points. Betty Rizzo has kindly shared with me results of her own research on Percy relatives and friends. I am grateful to Mr. and Mrs. Eric Brook, the Reverend N. E. Palmer, and the Reverend D. E. Havergal for their generous hospitality in Easton Mauduit and Wilby, and to Mary Hyde, Kenneth Balfour, and His Grace the Duke of Northumberland for similar hospitality in making their collections of Percy materials available to me. For assistance of various kinds my thanks go also to Hugh Amory, James Birchfield, Arthur Cash, J. D. Fleeman, Morris Golden, D. P. Graham, Donald Greene, Marjorie Hanson, J. F. A. Mason, Charles Miller, G. W. Nicholls, Stephen Parks, John Riely, John Shaw, Fred L. Standley, and W. Gordon Wheeler. A special note of appreciation must go to the Guggenheim Foundation for the fellowship which made possible the research for both this study and the biography with which I hope to follow it.

My debt to my wife will perhaps be suggested by my dedication of this study to her.

BERTRAM H. DAVIS

Florida State University

Chronology

1729   April 24, Thomas Percy born at Bridgnorth, Shropshire.

1741   Enrolls in Newport School under the Reverend Samuel Lea.

1746   July 7, matriculates at Christ Church College, Oxford.

1750   April 26, awarded bachelor of arts degree by Oxford.

1751   October 20, ordained a deacon; begins serving churches at Astley Abbots and Tasley in Shropshire.

1753   June 17, ordained a priest. July 5, awarded master of arts degree by Oxford. October 15, appointed vicar of Easton Mauduit in Northamptonshire. Begins keeping a pocket diary.

1756   April 21, takes up residence at Easton Mauduit. May 26, appointed chaplain to George Augustus Yelverton, earl of Sussex; August 4, made rector of Wilby. Makes acquaintance of Samuel Johnson.

1758   January 8, earl of Sussex dies. February 18, appointed chaplain to Henry Yelverton, earl of Sussex. Publishes first works: *Grand Magazine*, February (Latin poem) and March (two English poems).

1759   April 24, marries Anne Gutteridge.

1760   March 18, Anne Cleiveland Percy born.

1761   August 3, Barbara Percy born. November 14, *Hau Kiou Choaan*.

1762   May 28, *The Matrons*; December 13, *Miscellaneous Pieces Relating to the Chinese*.

1763   February 7, Henry Percy born. February 11, William Shenstone dies. April 2, *Five Pieces of Runic Poetry*.

1764   June 13, *The Song of Solomon*. June 25–August 18, Johnson spends seven weeks at Easton Mauduit.

1765   February 11, *Reliques of Ancient English Poetry*. Spring, appointed tutor to Algernon Percy and (June 28) chaplain to earl, later duke, of Northumberland. July 11, Elizabeth Percy born. Spends first summer at Alnwick Castle; *A Ride Round Hulne Abbey* privately printed.

1766   *A Key to the New Testament.*

1767   Second edition of *Reliques.* September 1, Charlotte Percy born. Mrs. Percy appointed wet nurse to Prince Edward.

1768   February 15, elected to the Club.

1769   November 24, appointed chaplain in ordinary to George III.

1770   June 8, *Northern Antiquities;* August 9, *A Sermon Preached before the Sons of the Clergy. Northumberland Houshold Book* privately printed. July 3, awarded doctor of divinity degree by Cambridge University. November 18, Anne Cleiveland Percy dies.

1771   January 9, Charlotte Percy dies. May 21, *The Hermit of Warkworth.*

1772   July 4, Hester Percy born.

1774   February 19, Hester Percy dies.

1775   Third edition of *Reliques.*

1776   December 7, duchess of Northumberland dies.

1778   April 12, altercation with Johnson over Pennant's comments on Alnwick Castle. November 16, appointed dean of Carlisle.

1779   Revised article on "Percy, Duke of Northumberland" published in Collins's *Peerage of England* (5th ed.).

1780   March 18, fire in Percy's apartment at Northumberland House.

1782   April 17, appointed bishop of Dromore.

1783   April 2, Henry Percy dies at Marseille. July, Percy family settles at Dromore.

1784   Article on John Cleiveland published in *Biographia Britannica* (2d ed.).

1786   June 1, elected fellow of Society of Antiquaries.

1790   *Sermon Preached at Christ-Church, Dublin.*

1793   July 3, awarded doctor of divinity degree by Oxford University.

1795   July, fourth edition of *Reliques* (dated 1794).

1801   *The Life of Dr. Oliver Goldsmith* published in Goldsmith's *Miscellaneous Works.*

Chronology

CHAPTER 1

Cleric and Scholar

WRITING to Thomas Percy in August, 1803, the Scottish physician and author, Robert Anderson, recalled that, just a year before, he had had the happiness of staying under Percy's roof in Northern Ireland, where Percy had been bishop of Dromore since 1782. "A visit to such a man," wrote Anderson, "like that of a pilgrim to a distant shrine, forms an era in the life of a private individual"; and he expressed satisfaction that he had helped to draw Percy out of his long retirement to resume his place "in the ranks of learning, and to receive renewed testimonies of public gratitude for... [his] eminent services to English poetry."[1]

The objects of such literary pilgrimages are usually the leading poets or novelists of the day, and no one could have asserted a place for Percy in either group. His prose fiction consisted of a little known translation of a Chinese novel and a less known collection of short tales about the frailty of widows, and his most ambitious poem fell like a stripling before the seasoned wit of Samuel Johnson's most famous parody. Yet Percy, without actually writing a great book, rose to eminence with one of the most revered and influential compilations of his time, the *Reliques of Ancient English Poetry*, and Anderson's citation of Percy's services to English poetry would have been echoed in the hearts of contemporaries everywhere. By 1802 the three-volume work published in 1765 was already familiarly known as *Percy's Reliques*, and, like Anderson, numerous other persons had found their way to Dromore to pay their respects to its learned and hospitable editor. Anderson's tribute was unusual only in its eloquence.

Percy's success with the *Reliques* seems almost ironic when one considers his frequently expressed attitude toward his work. A churchman from the outset of his professional life, he apolo-

15

gized in the first edition of the *Reliques* "for having bestowed . . . attention on a parcel of OLD BALLADS";[2] and as he advanced in clerical dignity and office he tended more and more to dismiss the *Reliques* as a youthful diversion undertaken merely to fill up the moments between important parochial duties. What troubled Percy in 1765, and perhaps throughout much of his life, was that, in the minds of his contemporaries, the ballads were identified with the broadsides that poured in profusion from the garrets and stalls of Grub Street—acceptable amusements, perhaps, but hardly meriting serious pursuit by a conscientious divine. "I bestow upon a few old poems," Percy wrote to Lord Hailes on January 25, 1763, "those idle moments, which some of my grave brethren pass away over a sober game at whist."[3] Percy proved, of course, to be oversensitive on this point. The combining of clerical and literary careers was a commonplace of the eighteenth century, as it had been earlier, and clergymen did not always limit their efforts to subjects of unquestioned delicacy. Jonathan Swift held the deanship of St. Patrick's Cathedral while he was obtruding the yahoos upon a complacent public. And many of Percy's friends—his Northamptonshire neighbor Edward Lye, for example, who compiled an Anglo-Saxon dictionary, and such men at the universities as Thomas Warton and Richard Farmer— were accomplished scholars who, far from suggesting that old ballads were beneath a clergyman's notice, gave Percy every possible assistance with them. It was Percy's abilities rather than his pursuits that set him apart from his contemporaries.

I *Early Life*

Percy, who changed the spelling of his name from Piercy to Percy in 1756, was born in Bridgnorth, Shropshire, on April 24, 1729, the eldest of three sons of a wholesale grocer and tobacconist, Arthur Lowe Piercy, who had married Jane Nott in 1727.[4] The Piercys lived in a handsome three-gabled tudor house in the Cartway which still catches the visitor's eye as he crosses the bridge from the low town to the high town. Arthur Lowe Piercy served at various times as magistrate and alderman in Bridgnorth, and distinguished himself, according to his son, by the vigor with which he invoked the laws against the keepers of disorderly houses, which were "supported & openly protected by some Rakes of great fortune in the neighborhood."[5]

Young Thomas began his studies in the Bridgnorth Free School but made little progress. In the spring of 1741 he was sent to Newport School in Shropshire, where in 1726 an effort to secure Samuel Johnson a place as a student assistant to the headmaster had been unsuccessful; and after five years, though still "of the third Class from the top,"[6] Percy was elected an exhibitioner to Christ Church College, Oxford, on the newly established Careswell Foundation. In view of some recent financial reverses of his father, this scholarship assistance proved very timely, and on July 7, 1746, he was entered a commoner at Christ Church and placed under the tutelage of the Reverend Richard Hind. An exceptional student, Percy received the further honor on November 3, 1747, of being chosen one of Bishop Fell's exhibitioners.

Percy graduated on April 26, 1750, but stayed on at Oxford to study Hebrew and to complete other requirements for the master's degree. He was ordained a deacon at Hereford on October 20, 1751, and for the next four and a half years served as deacon and curate in the two churches of Astley Abbots and Tasley, just outside of Bridgnorth. He was ordained a priest on June 17, 1753, and the next month was awarded the master's degree by the university. On October 15 of that year the dean and chapter of Christ Church appointed him vicar of Easton Mauduit in Northamptonshire, but he did not take up residence in Easton Mauduit until April, 1756; and shortly thereafter his patron at Easton Mauduit, George Augustus Yelverton, earl of Sussex, made him his chaplain and presented him with an additional living as rector of nearby Wilby. Percy was to hold both church appointments until he became bishop of Dromore in 1782.

Percy's congregations in Shropshire and Northamptonshire were small, and they made few demands upon his time. Between them, during his four and a half years, the churches at Astley Abbots and Tasley had only sixty-six baptisms, thirty-one burials, and fourteen weddings, and Percy did not officiate at all of them.[7] In 1757, a fairly typical year, the churches at Easton Mauduit and Wilby had only three baptisms, twelve burials, and two weddings, an average of one function every three weeks in addition to the services he regularly conducted at one church

on Sunday mornings and at the other on Sunday evenings.[8] He
was, to be sure, called upon now and then to substitute for neigh-
boring clergymen who, for one reason or another, were unable
to fulfill their engagements, and of course there were parish
duties which he never mentioned in his letters or diaries: a
"perambulation" of Easton Mauduit parish, for example, joined
in by old and young on May 17, 1757.[9] But he seems to have
been free to use much of his time exactly as he wished.

Never one to remain idle, Percy spent hours over his books,
and by the time of his move to Easton Mauduit he had already
assembled a creditable library. The first of his extant pocket
diaries dates from 1753, and it was probably during this period
in Shropshire that he came into possession of the manuscript
that was to form the basis of the *Reliques of Ancient English
Poetry*. In the early and mid-1750s he tried his hand at poetical
translations, particularly of Ovid, and he wrote a number of
playful love poems to young women—renamed for the occasion
Flavia, Cynthia, Delia, Mira—who seemed to enjoy his company
as much as he enjoyed theirs. Most of his first published works
were poems. He had, in fact, a bit of the dandy in him and took
pleasure in reviewing his prospects at neighborhood dances and
other social events. He was fond also of gardening and of culti-
vating his glebe lands, and on one afternoon during his second
year at Easton Mauduit he was the delighted beneficiary of an
unscheduled outdoor entertainment. "Last Week," he wrote to
his cousin William Cleiveland on June 25, 1757,

I mow'd my little Vicarage-Close, & some Ladies were so good as to
come & help me to make Hay:—When tir'd with ye Heat & Toil of
the day, upon no other velvet Couch than a soft & fragrant Hay-Cock,
with the Canopy of a spreading Ash, we sat down to drink Tea, and
spent the afternoon in the most lively & chatty manner. . . .[10]

He was also steadily widening his circle of literary friends.
The first letter in his correspondence with the physician and
poet James Grainger dates from 1756, and the first surviving
letter to the poet William Shenstone from 1757. From Easton
Mauduit he often undertook the day's journey to London, where
Grainger introduced him to Samuel Johnson late in 1756 and

to Oliver Goldsmith on February 21, 1759. He called on both Johnson and Goldsmith frequently during his London visits and seems to have brought the two formally together when he escorted Johnson to a dinner at Goldsmith's lodgings on May 31, 1761.[11] By the summer of 1764 he and Johnson were on such intimate terms that Johnson, accompanied by the blind Anna Williams spent seven weeks with the Percys in the Easton Mauduit vicarage.

On April 24, 1759, Percy celebrated his thirtieth birthday by marrying Anne Gutteridge, the subject of his best-known poem, "O Nancy, wilt thou go with me." If marriage put an end to grand balls and to afternoon teas in the haycock, it brought Percy the far more vital fulfillment to which they had been pointing: a son who survived long enough to become a university student; five daughters, two of whom outlived both Percy and his wife; and above all a genuine happiness that endured until Mrs. Percy's death in 1806. "I must ascribe," wrote Percy to his wife on their wedding anniversary in 1799, "a great Deal of the Happiness as well as Prosperity of my Life to your Love & Tenderness in every exigence, & to your Prudence & Oeconomy.— In our earlier years how excellently did you manage our little revenue."[12]

II *Middle Years*

Although the little revenue of the young Percy family did not quickly ripen into affluence, Percy's diligence, learning, and affability steadily brought other rewards. The decade between 1761 and 1771 may in fact be looked upon as his miraculous years, for they saw the publication of all ten of his books, a sermon, a long descriptive letter, and a second edition of the *Reliques of Ancient English Poetry*.[13] His first book, a four-volume edition of the Chinese novel *Hau Kiou Choaan*, was published in November, 1761, and was quickly followed by *The Matrons* and *Miscellaneous Pieces Relating to the Chinese* (both 1762), *Five Pieces of Runic Poetry* (1763), and *The Song of Solomon* (1764). In 1764 Percy was granted permission to dedicate the *Reliques* to Elizabeth, countess of Northumberland; and he was appointed tutor to Algernon Percy, her younger son, in the spring of 1765 and chaplain to the earl of Northumberland on June 28 of that year, less than five months after the publication of the *Reliques*. Doubtless this close connection with the influential Northumberland family—the earl became the duke of Northumberland in 1766—also led to Mrs. Percy's designation in 1767 as wet nurse to the infant Prince Edward, who was to be the father of Queen Victoria, and to Percy's own appointments as chaplain in ordinary to George III in 1769 and dean of Carlisle Cathedral in 1778. From 1765 until 1782, when he became bishop of Dromore, Percy was allotted an apartment in Northumberland House, the duke's palatial home at Charing Cross in London, and he annually accompanied the duke and duchess on their summer jaunts to Alnwick Castle, just a few miles from the Northumberland coast.

In 1770 Cambridge University awarded him the doctor of divinity degree, an honor that Oxford also conferred upon him in 1793. A significant literary recognition came in 1768 when, with the expansion to twelve members of the famous literary club ("The Club") founded by Johnson and others in 1764, Percy was admitted to membership along with the lawyer and magistrate Robert Chambers and the dramatist George Colman. He was one of the most constant attendants at the weekly club meetings when he was in London, and was able through the club to cultivate his friendships with Johnson and Goldsmith and to form close attachments with such other members as Sir Joshua Reynolds and the Shakespearean scholar Edmond Malone. These were years also of association with James Boswell, who recalled him vividly if not always flatteringly in the *Life of Johnson*, most memorably in a heated dispute with Johnson over Thomas Pennant's published remarks about Alnwick Castle. "Upon my honour, Sir, I did not mean to be uncivil," said Percy as they began to make up. "I cannot say so, Sir," replied Johnson; "for I *did* mean to be uncivil, thinking *you* had been uncivil."[14]

By the time of his appointment as dean of Carlisle, most of Percy's literary work was behind him. *A Key to the New Testament* was published in 1766, the *Northumberland Houshold Book* and *Northern Antiquities* in 1770, Percy's original ballad *The Hermit of Warkworth* in 1771, and a third edition of the *Reliques* in 1775. Editions of Surrey's poems and Buckingham's works, undertaken as early as 1761, were languishing at the printer's, where they were to be almost totally destroyed by a fire that consumed John Nichols's warehouse in February, 1808. A revision of the article on "Percy, Duke of Northumberland" in Collins's *Peerage of England* was nearing completion and would be published in Collins's fifth edition in 1779. But other projects were either turned over to new editors or quietly abandoned, including one—translations from the Spanish entitled *Ancient Songs Chiefly on Moorish Subjects*—for which copperplates had been engraved and the title page printed. Plainly the responsibilities of vicarage, rectorate, chaplaincies, and deanship, all held concurrently, were sufficient even for one of Percy's capacities, and, a good churchman always, he turned away from literary relaxations and fixed his course along the path of duty.

III   *Last Years*

Percy became the bishop of Dromore, not through the duke of Northumberland's influence but because the prelate who was offered the bishopric preferred to be dean of Carlisle and Percy wished to be a bishop.[15] So a trade was arranged, and Percy, appointed by letter of the king on April 17, 1782, left for Dromore in May, 1782, to meet some of his new constituents and to survey his duties and his estate. The Irish were enthusiastic and generous; with a name to precede him, the editor of the *Reliques* was given an author's as well as a bishop's welcome. Mrs. Percy reported to William Cleiveland on June 12 that "Numbers of the first fashion have been to pay their respects to your Cousin, as well as Bishops," and that her husband had dined at home only four times since his arrival in Ireland.[16] Percy himself informed Cleiveland after his return to England that he had had an "agreeable Tour" through Ireland and had visited about half his churches. Unfortunately, he added, the newly built bishop's palace was not yet dry enough to be moved into, and the Percy family would thus be compelled to stay in England until the following spring.[17] It was actually July before they settled into their new home.

One so closely identified as Percy with leading English clerics, poets, and scholars might have been expected to look upon a bishopric in remote Dromore as little better than exile. But Percy had an extraordinary ability to find happiness wherever he went. In the tiny village of Easton Mauduit he had enjoyed his house and garden, his clerical friends in nearby villages, and his association with the earl of Sussex and (though somewhat less) the earl's brother, who succeeded to the title in 1758; he had reached out of his parochial circle by constant reading, occasional trips to London, and a voluminous correspondence with friends and scholars in all parts of Britain. After 1765, when he divided his time among Easton Mauduit, London, and Alnwick, he settled into the Northumberland household almost as a member of the family: a secretary as well as a chaplain whom the duke and duchess at times found indispensable. For the aspiring Percy a connection with one of England's great families was a satisfaction in itself. That it should be with a family of his own name gave it a special attraction, and stimulated his inquiries into the history of the Northumberland Percys and his own suspected links with them. In the deanship of Carlisle he found numerous satisfactions also, and characteristically he made friends among both his fellow clergy and the laity, and set about converting the deanery into a residence after his own taste.

It was no different at Dromore, far as it was from the excitement of London and the Club and from the friends of a busy and rewarding three decades. His garden became a passion, and he doted upon the children born to his daughters Barbara and Elizabeth. He entered enthusiastically into the activities of Irish intellectual societies and sent occasional notes to the *Gentleman's Magazine* on matters of scientific or literary interest. In spite of a failing eyesight which in 1804 culminated in almost total blindness, he kept up a steady correspondence with Edmond Malone, Robert Anderson, the poetess Jane West, and others almost to the day of his death. At Anderson's request he supplied extensive notes for the third edition of Anderson's *Life of Johnson* and for the life and works of James Grainger; and with great difficulty he prodded into life an edition of Goldsmith's *Miscellaneous Works,* for which he penned the life of Goldsmith which introduces it. The security of his literary reputation was threatened only by the persistent assaults of Joseph Ritson upon his editorial practices in the *Reliques,* but he managed to blunt their effect at least in his own lifetime.

As a churchman, Percy insisted that his clergy recognize that their first duty was to their parishioners, and he took pride in the Sunday schools that distinguished his diocese.[18] Inevitably church responsibilities, including attendance at the annual sessions of the Irish Parliament, held him very largely in Ireland. He returned to England in 1791, however, so that Mrs. Percy's health might benefit from the waters at Bath, and again in 1795 after his cousin William Cleiveland had left him his entire estate and when the publication of a fourth edition of the *Reliques* was imminent. His last visit was in 1800, a long-awaited rejoining of his family, sent to England for safety while he remained in Ireland during the rebellion of 1798 and the grueling political activity which preceded the vote for Anglo-Irish union in 1800. He died at Dromore on September 30, 1811, respected and even loved as a prelate, but celebrated still as the editor of the *Reliques of Ancient English Poetry.*

CHAPTER 2

A Poetic Apprenticeship

IT was fortunate that of Percy's two passions in literature—
poetry and antiquity—his love of poetry came first, and that
for some years his creative spirit settled upon the writing of
short poems and the translation of Latin classics. For if Percy
was not to leave a discernible mark as a poet, he was nonetheless
developing a feeling for poetic form and content, for language,
imagery, and rhythm, that was to transmute the best of his
antiquarian work. Distinguishing Percy from the "mere antiquarian," Samuel Johnson noted in 1778 that Percy's attention
to poetry had given "grace and splendour to his studies of antiquity."[1] Through Percy's alchemy, the "parcel of OLD BALLADS"
was displayed to the public with much of the luster of polished
gold, and, whatever Percy's own misgivings, scholars since his
time have not hesitated to ransack the ballad literature for the
innumerable treasures that Percy gave them reason to hope they
would find.

I First Efforts

Percy's earliest extant poems date from the period 1752–1754,
when he was a young curate at Astley Abbots and Tasley in
Shropshire. Addressed mainly to young ladies of his acquaintance,
they have little to recommend them, and not surprisingly few
of them have found their way into print. An exception of particular interest is a 1752 epigram in imitation of Alexander Pope,
which was set aside for *Shenstone's Miscellany* and not published
until 1952, for it suggests a somewhat specialized poetic talent
which Percy was to make extensive use of in the *Reliques*. One
of Pope's numerous witticisms at the expense of Poet Laureate
Colley Cibber was the following:

> In merry old England it once was a rule,
> The King had his Poet, and also his Fool:
> But now we're so frugal, I'd have you to know it,
> That *Cibber* can serve both for Fool and for Poet.[2]

Witty though it is, the epigram is not one of Pope's happier efforts. It is written in such general terms, and with such dependence on forms of *to be* and *to have*, that it fails to create a vivid picture, and through its facile rhyme of "know it" and "poet" it ends in a patent banality. Its interest, of course, centers in its joining of the king's poet and fool in one person, and it is this idea that Percy, avoiding the faults of Pope's epigram, adapts in a poem that Pope might not have been displeased to own:

> At the Squire's long board, in the days of Queen Bess
> Sate the Fool to make sport, & the chaplain to bless.
> But frugal Sir Flint has contracted the Rule
> And Bibo's to serve both for Chaplain—and Fool.[3]

Had Percy been able to dress his own ideas as colorfully, the whole course of his life might have been much different. A quick glance at "The Disappointment," however—a poem addressed to an unidentified Mira and published in two versions in the 1952 *Shenstone's Miscellany*—suggests how inept Percy could be when left to his own devices. In 1752 Percy opened the poem with the following stanza:

> Mira, the toast of half our sex,
> Whose blooming cheeks dame Venus decks
>   With roses and with Lillies:
> Who looks a Goddess, moves a Queen:
> And if she sings, how clearly seen
>   The Muses sweetest skill is?

In his 1753 version, Percy changed *sings* to *sing* in line five and *sweetest* to *tunefull* in line six, but he clung to the rhyme of "Lillies" and "skill is," as he did to "seas 'em" and "freeze 'em" in the poem's final stanza.[4]

It is hard to believe that the imitation of Pope's epigram and "The Disappointment" were written in the same year by the same person: the one was wit and the other doggerel barely aspiring to be wit. The public, one may surmise, was not unduly inconvenienced by the 200-year delay in the publication of "The Disappointment"; had it viewed the poem in 1753, it might reasonably have concluded that Percy had no demonstrable future as a poet. His pursuit of the muse, however, appears to have paralleled his pursuit of the young ladies of Shropshire and nearby counties. On May 25, 1756, he dined in London with his cousin Mary Perrins and delivered two sonnets to her son-in-law Richard Rolt, an editor of the *Universal Visiter*.[5] One of them, "A Sonnet, after the Manner of Spencer, Address'd to a Lady," was published in the May, 1756, issue of the *Universal Visiter*, and since the lady addressed is "fair Anna" it has been natural to think of her as Percy's future wife, Anne Gutteridge. But in his copy of Anna Williams's *Miscellanies in Prose and Verse*, where the poem was reprinted in 1766 under the title "A Sonnet to a Lady of Indiscreet Virtue," Percy identified Anna as "Miss Cotton of Bridgnorth." He also dated the poem "about 1754."[6] Anna's quality of outgoing innocence is captured with some success in the opening stanza:

> While you, fair *Anna,* innocently gay,
>   And free, and open, all reserve disdain;
> Where-ever Fancy leads, securely stray,
>   And conscious of no ill can fear no stain.[7]

The second sonnet was published in the July, 1756, issue and, according to the title, was occasioned by Percy's leaving Bath in June, 1755. Addressed to "the Misses H***," it informs these "fair ones" that his departure from Bath is a "Far heavier doom" than Adam's departure from Eden, for Adam had Eve to "raise, with converse sweet, the drooping mind," whereas he is leaving "of nymphs so fair, a train behind."[8] Percy's analogy inevitably invites speculation about his conduct among the ladies of Bath, but his tribute—inflated rather than inspired—was hardly made to withstand the mischief of intensive analysis.

II   *Songs and Elegies*

In February, 1758, Percy's friend James Grainger invited him to contribute to the *Grand Magazine,* a new monthly sponsored among others by the printer William Strahan and Ralph Griffiths of the *Monthly Review,* who, as Grainger wrote, "have often heard me praise your poetical talents."[9] The editors had requested the Scottish version of a Percy poem entitled "Song" and beginning "O Nancy, wilt thou go with me," which Grainger had been shown in manuscript, but they settled for a twelve-line Latin poem and the two sonnets published earlier in the *Universal Visiter.*[10] Rather curiously, in the *Grand Magazine* printing of the second sonnet, the Misses H*** became mere "ladies," while Bath was altered to B–R–T–N and June, 1755, to July, 1755, changes which would seem to reflect either on Percy's memory or on his constancy if one did not have the more likely explanation that the sonnet was an exercise rather than a lyric intended for precise application. On April 4, 1758, Grainger informed Percy that his "Hints to the Poets" would be published in the next issue, but nothing with that title was published, and only an essay in the May, 1759, issue ("Observations on the Complexion of the Times") comes at all close to suiting Grainger's title.

Perhaps Percy did not send the *Grand Magazine* his Scotch song, as Grainger called it, because he had already given Robert Dodsley an English version of it for his *Collection of Poems,* a new edition of which was published in March, 1758. The song appeared in volume 6 of Dodsley's *Collection,* along with "Cynthia, an Elegiac Poem," an inconsequential attempt by Percy to imitate the style of Gray's *Elegy.*[11] Although the Scottish version requested by the editors antedated the English, it does not appear to have been published until 1787, when James Johnson printed it in the *Scots Musical Museum* with a musical setting by Joseph Baildon. The English version was set to music by Thomas Carter about 1770.[12] Of the two poetic versions, the English understandably proved the more enduring, and it has been frequently reprinted. A writer in the *Gentleman's Magazine* for August, 1780—probably Joseph Warton—described it as "tender, easy, and elegant,"[13] and Percy's contemporary John Aiken thought that it had "scarcely its equal for real tenderness in this or any other language."[14] Robert Burns called it "perhaps, the most beautiful Ballad in the English language." As for the Scottish version, which he did not know to be Percy's own work, Burns thought it "too barefaced to take Dr. Percy's charming song, and by the means of transposing a few English words into Scots, to offer to pass it for a Scots song."[15]

Burns may have mistaken the sinner, but he did not mistake the sin. Percy's Scotticisms are superficial adornments that do not conceal the poem's basic English fabric, as may be seen by examining the variants in the English and Scottish versions:

O Nancy, wilt thou go with me,   (Annie!; gang wi')
    Nor sigh to leave the flaunting town:
Can silent glens have charms for thee,   (hae)
    The lowly cot and russet gown?
No longer dress'd in silken sheen,   (Nae langer)
    No longer deck'd with jewels rare,   (Nae langer; wi')
Say can'st thou quit each courtly scene,
    Where thou wert fairest of the fair?

O Nancy! when thou'rt far away,   (Annie!; awa')
    Wilt thou not cast a wish behind?
Say canst thou face the parching ray,   (flaky snaw)
    Nor shrink before the wintry wind?
O can that soft and gentle mien   (saft)
    Extremes of hardship learn to bear.
Nor sad regret each courtly scene,
    Where thou wert fairest of the fair?

O Nancy! can'st thou love so true   (sae)
    Thro' perils keen with me to go,   (wi'; gae)
Or when thy swain mishap shall rue,
    To share with him the pang of woe?   (wae)
Say should disease or pain befal,
    Wilt thou assume the nurse's care,
Nor wistful those gay scenes recall
    Where thou wert fairest of the fair?

And when at last thy love shall die,
    Wilt thou receive his parting breath?
Wilt thou repress each struggling sigh,
    And chear with smiles the bed of death?   (wi')
And wilt thou o'er his breathless clay
    Strew flow'rs, and drop the tender tear,
Nor *then* regret those scenes so gay,   (sae)
    Where thou wert fairest of the fair?[16]

The differences, in short, are only in the names of Nancy and Annie, in ten words (four of them used more than once), and in the substitution of "flaky snaw" for "parching ray" to meet the need for a rhyme in the second stanza. In words, and perhaps even more in spirit, the lines are a long way from the Scottish tradition exemplified in such poets as Allan Ramsay:

> My *Peggy* smiles sae kindly,
> It makes me blyth and bauld.
> And naithing gi'es me sic delight,
> As wawking of the fauld.[17]

What seems likely is that Percy, who had a bookish rather than a practical knowledge of the Scottish dialect, wrote the poem first in English and then adapted it to the Scottish manner of song-writing as he perceived it. It is interesting to find in this connection that, in December, 1761, when Percy's friend Shenstone was writing to John McGowan in Edinburgh, Percy transcribed his Scottish version on the second leaf of the letter and noted that M[r]. Shenstone is to add some Scotticisms,"[18] as though Percy was acknowledging the transparency of the decorative Scottish cover he had himself provided.

"O Nancy" was clearly Percy's best-liked poem—not the most beautiful ballad in the English language, to be sure, and not a poem with scarcely an equal for real tenderness in any language, but one which, on the whole, merited the more restrained tribute of Joseph Warton. It is tender and easy and at times elegant. It has the simplicity of the Scots song if not its lightness of touch: it is pathetic rather than playful. It is also a little self-pitying and melodramatic as it puts Nancy presumptuously to the test of imagining herself a widow; and one or two of its lines are pedestrian at best, so that it does not always sing when it should: "Or when thy swain mishap shall rue,/ To share with him the pang of woe?" But its opening and closing lines stay with one and make it always a temptation to call the poem "O Nancy! wilt thou go with me" or "The Fairest of the Fair." Most of all, it manages to convey a feeling of genuine love. Percy's ultimate celebration of Nancy, it is inseparable from Anne Gutteridge—Anne Percy—and quite rightly appears in the only

known portrait of her, just as the folio manuscript appears in
Sir Joshua Reynolds's lost portrait of her husband.

As a poet Percy was understandably moved to his best efforts
by his future wife. One of his most effective poems was "Verses
on leaving **** in a tempestuous night; March 22, 1758," which
was set aside for *Shenstone's Miscellany* and apparently not published in Percy's lifetime. As the storm "Deep howls" outside,
Percy forcefully describes the power of love to draw him away
from "The chearfull blaze, the social hour, / The Friend" and
"to dare this hideous night" of snow, rain, and wind to be with
his love, called Delia in *Shenstone's Miscellany* but identified as
Anne in Percy's manuscript:

> Love bids atchieve the hardy Deed
> And act the wonderous part[;]
> He wings the foot with eagle-speed
> And lends the Lion-heart[.][19]

In addition to short love poems, Percy devoted a good deal
of time to Latin translations, particularly of Ovid's *Epistles,*
which in 1759 James Grainger tried without success to interest
Dodsley or Andrew Millar in publishing. No doubt the publication of a translation by the Reverend Stephen Barrett in January
of that year was a formidable obstacle for still another translator to overcome. Percy returned intermittently to his task,
however, and as late as February 16, 1767, was inviting William
Cleiveland to join him in finishing the *Epistles*; but if Percy by
then lacked time for the project, Cleiveland apparently lacked
his cousin's enthusiasm, and nothing came of the proposal.[20]
Percy's only published Latin translations were an elegy of
Tibullus and Ovid's elegy on the death of Tibullus, both of them
in Grainger's *Poetical Translation of the Elegies of Tibullus.*
Grainger's volume appeared late in 1758, although its title page
bears the date 1759.

In his initial letter to Percy, written on October 22, 1756,
Grainger called for Percy's translation of Tibullus's first elegy,
which presumably had been undertaken at Grainger's request.
In February, 1758, he asked to have Percy's translation of Ovid's
elegy on Tibullus "by the first opportunity," and he noted the

opinion of Percy's friend the Reverend Robert Binnel that the
translation was "both exact and elegant." "It will be a great
ornament to the Life," wrote Grainger.[21] Clearly Percy's part
in the book, which also included emendations of some of
Grainger's translations, was considerable, and Grainger acknowledged it handsomely in the "Advertisement" printed at the beginning of his volume:

the Translator must return his sincere thanks to a worthy Friend,
for his elegant Version of the First Elegy, and of Ovid's Poem on
the Death of Tibullus. By what Accident his own Translation of the
first Elegy was lost, is of no consequence; especially too, as the
Reader, from a Perusal of Mr. P***'s Specimen, will probably be
induced to wish, that more of those now published, had undergone
a like Fate, provided the same Gentleman had likewise translated
them.[22]

Percy's two translations, like "Cynthia, an Elegiac Poem" and
his translations of Ovid's *Epistles*, were written in the four-line
stanza popularized by Thomas Gray in the *Elegy Written in a
Country Church-Yard*. No less a person than Tobias Smollett,
while reviewing the Tibullus volume unfavorably in the *Critical
Review*, singled out the "alternate stanza" for praise in contrast
to Grainger's heroic couplets, and also—perhaps with a mischievous glance at Grainger's "Advertisement"—pointedly commended the Percy translation of Ovid's elegy.[23] No doubt Percy
found the praise of his own work gratifying, but the invidious
comparison with Grainger must have caused him some embarrassment, particularly since Grainger was sufficiently disturbed by
Smollett's criticism to reply publicly in *A Letter to Tobias Smollet, M.D.*[24]

Smollett's comments notwithstanding, the twenty-three stanzas
of Percy's Ovid and the thirty-one of his Tibullus call for no
special attention. They are neither much better nor much worse
than many of the translations which fill up the poetry corners
of eigheenth-century periodicals, and, like other elegiac poems
of the time, they derive much from Milton (and something from
Pope and Gray also) without acquiring any distinctive quality
of their own:

Still live, the Work of Ages, Ilion's Fame,
   And the slow Web by nightly Craft unwove:
So Nemesis' shall live, and Delia's Name;
   This his first Passion, that his recent Love.[25]

Perhaps Percy himself had some misgivings about them. His
pride of authorship was not so keen, in any event, that he could
not abandon the translator's role at one point and simply incorporate a stanza from an elegy of James Hammond, of whom
Johnson was to write in his *Lives of the Poets*, "His verses are
not rugged, but they have no sweetness; they never glide in a
stream of melody." The remark fits Percy's translations equally
well. As for the stanza form, much as Johnson admired Gray's
Elegy he could only ask why "Hammond or other writers have
thought the quatrain of ten syllables elegiac" and leave the
question unanswered.[26] Percy's view, expressed in a letter to
Shenstone dated January 9, 1758, was that the quatrain was so
"peculiarly suited to the plaintive turn of Elegy" that he was
given "great offence" whenever he saw any other verse form
"applied" to it.[27]

On May 4, 1761, Percy wrote to Ralph Griffiths, former editor
of the *Grand Magazine* who was then publishing *The Library:
or Moral and Critical Magazine*, to say that he could not judge
how far he could contribute to Griffiths's new publication without
seeing it. He promised, however, to look among his papers, which
included Hebrew criticisms and dissertations, notes on classical
authors, anecdotes of eminent persons, "&c. &c &c," all of which,
he assured Griffiths, had at least the merit of being original.
For the moment, he was submitting a prayer drawn up three
years earlier for Anne Gutteridge when she was preparing to be
inoculated for smallpox on the advice of James Grainger.[28] Griffiths published the prayer anonymously in the May issue of *The
Library*, and in an unsigned introductory note Percy expressed
the hope that it would help to remove "the scruples of many
well-meaning, but weak people, who look upon inoculation as
an impious practice."[29] A prolix and at times prosaic effort, the
prayer is an interesting reminder nonetheless that inoculation
seemed almost as dreadful to the eighteenth century as the disease itself: "O strengthen and support me during this alarming

trial; soften the pains, and abate the violence of the disorder;
... be pleased to hearken to the prayers of my friends for me
every where...."

Griffiths can be forgiven if he did not respond enthusiastically
to Percy's offer to go rummaging through his stockpile. Even
original Hebrew criticisms and dissertations were not likely to
do much for a magazine's circulation. Percy did send Griffiths
an article on "Popish Relics" and a burlesque epistle on a country
schoolmaster, but the first of these was held up through the
carelessness of another of Griffiths's writers, and the magazine
expired in 1762 before either could be published.[30] Percy had
better luck a year later, when he was able to contribute original,
and new, verses in English to a publication which seemed assured
of a substantial circulation.

III   *Stonhouse's* Friendly Advice

Percy's "Stanzas Occasioned by Dr. Stonhouse's *Friendly Advice to a Patient*" was first published in 1762 in the ninth edition
of that very popular pamphlet. Since the pamphlet continued
to be reprinted and was sold in lots of a hundred for two
guineas by the Society for Promoting Christian Knowledge, this
was doubtless the most widely distributed early Percy poem, and
its distribution was given a further impetus when it was reprinted
in the *Scots* and *Gentleman's* magazines for November, 1762.[31]

The physician Sir James Stonhouse was the founder of the
Northampton Infirmary, for which Percy preached a charity
sermon on September 22, 1758.[32] Probably their acquaintance
began shortly after Percy's move to Easton Mauduit in 1756, but
their earliest exchange of letters dates from the summer of 1762,
when Stonhouse confessed some embarrassment to Percy over
a line in Moses Browne's poetic tribute in the eighth edition of
Friendly Advice: "Great and good Man! by Heaven blest." "I am
far from being Great," wrote Stonhouse, who was soon to give
up medicine for the church, "& not very good I can tell you."
In reply, Percy let it be known that he had always thought
Browne's poem "a fulsome, poor performance, & no credit to
your book."[33]

Percy's was not a fulsome, poor performance, and, without

pretensions itself, it may be considered a credit to Dr. Stonhouse's unpretentious little tract. In its nine six-line stanzas it
welcomes the approach to health through the Christian life—
through the preservation of the spirit as well as of the body; and
it commends both the hospital for its care of the sick cottager
who otherwise "had died obscure" and the cottager's "generous
Friend" for attempting "the nobler Part": "For see while Medicine makes the Body whole, / This little Tract affords Prescrip-
tions for the Soul."

Before the appearance of the ninth edition, Dr. Stonhouse
submitted Percy's poem to a few friends, and he sent Percy their
suggestions, most of which had come from a man named Nixon
at Cold Higham. Nixon found fault with "rack the race" in the
fourth stanza, which he said sounds "uncouthly"; with the use
of the word "say" three times in four stanzas; and with the final
line of the poem, which he declared is "not grammar."[34] He also
suggested that the last words of the line "That make him loath
Life's little Span" be changed to "Life's scanty span" to avoid
the alliteration.

Percy made one or two changes when he returned the poem
to Dr. Stonhouse, but he rejected Nixon's suggestions with some
vehemence:

You say "Nixon pronounces the last line *not* grammar." If he does,
I pronounce him hasty and inconsiderate. He forgets that *true poetry*
delights in bold figures, and loves to drop an obvious word for the
imagination to supply. . . .
Remember, that a graceful negligence, if accompanied with beauty,
is in poetry, infinitely preferable to a tame and faultless insipidity. . . .
Was I to make all the alterations recommended in your friends papers,
. . . I should drain my small poem of whatever little spirit it chances
to be possest. . . .

"What think you of *life's scanty span?*" he asked Dr. Stonhouse.
There's "a fine hissing dissonant cluster of consonants," and all to
avoid the alliteration, which "was here studied, and is a beauty."
And the same critic, he chided, "counts over his fingers how
often a word or a letter has been used in the poem. . . . A fine
mechanical way of wit!"[35]

If ten years of versifying had not made Percy a poet, they had at least helped to make him an astute critic. He perceived that much of the delight of poetry came from the stimulus given to the imagination by the unusual and the unexpected, and that to judge poetry in a purely mechanical way, as Nixon judged a conscious repetition, was to bring a plebeian mind to a patrician task. He was keenly attuned also to the music of poetry, and he cringed at the harsh absurdity of Nixon's "hissing dissonant cluster of consonants" proposed as an alternative to the liquidity of his own alliteration. "How dare you call Pope a bungler for coupling *draught* and *brought?*" he wrote to Stonhouse in defense of his own rhyming of *Draught* and *unbought* in the sixth stanza of the poem: "You are a bold man, and cannot but know that he had the most correct & delicate ear in the world.—In short, in whatever regards versification & rhime, his authority is most absolute and decisive. Dryden is sometimes careless in this respect, but Pope never."[36]

Perhaps Percy's six-years' association with Samuel Johnson had helped to bring him to this conviction of the relative care taken of their poems by Dryden and Pope, for Percy's comparison of Pope's correctness with Dryden's occasional carelessness brings to mind the more comprehensive analysis of the two poets that was to distinguish Johnson's *Life of Pope* almost two decades later. But whatever their background, these are the comments of a thoughtful critic who had benefited much by steeping himself in poetry, not merely by constant reading but by frequent writing also. It was just the kind of apprenticeship one might have prescribed for the future editor of the *Reliques of Ancient English Poetry*.

CHAPTER 3

"I find you are indefatigable"

PERCY'S intense interest in poetry was matched by his interest in learning, and at Easton Mauduit he found conditions almost ideal for the pursuit of the scholar's life. The unbelievably light demands of his two churches left him with hours and even days on end to do with as he pleased. His patron and near neighbor, the young George Augustus Yelverton, 16th earl of Sussex, opened his library to him and offered him companionship as well as encouragement; and after the earl's untimely death in 1758 at the age of thirty, his brother, Henry, though less companionable, continued to grant Percy access to the library. The Anglo-Saxon scholar Edward Lye, rector of Yardley Hastings just a few miles away, became a close friend. A few hours' journey could take him to William Shenstone at the Leasowes, and in a day's time he could be in London, where over a three-year span he became closely attached to James Grainger, Samuel Johnson, and Oliver Goldsmith. A pen which often turned out half a dozen lengthy letters a day helped him to cultivate the friendships of other scholars like Thomas Warton, Richard Farmer, Evan Evans, and David Dalrymple, who responded to his enthusiasm and generosity by supplying him with information and suggestions and sometimes with books and manuscripts.

"I find you are indefatigable," Evan Evans wrote to Percy on April 17, 1765, with an accuracy that all of Percy's scholarly friends would have appreciated.[1] Percy's pursuit of his objectives was relentless, and his letters brim over with facts and argument, with questions and requests, with titles, allusions, and quotations. Such energy not only helped to catapult a young and obscure country vicar and rector into the company of the leading scholars and writers of the day; within the space of six years it secured for him a series of publishers' contracts probably

36

unequaled for sheer ambition in the annals of English literature. On March 8, 1759, he received twenty-five pounds from Robert Dodsley for a translation of a Chinese novel that was nearing completion. He reached agreements with Dodsley on May 21, 1761, for proposed translations of *The Song of Solomon* and *Five Pieces of Runic Poetry*; on May 22, 1761, for the *Reliques of Ancient English Poetry*; and on May 23, 1761, for *The Matrons* and *Miscellaneous Pieces Relating to the Chinese*. He contracted with Jacob Tonson on June 12, 1761, to edit the works of Buckingham; on March 24, 1763, to edit Surrey's poems; on May 25, 1764, to edit *The Guardian* and *The Spectator*; and on March 16, 1765, to edit *The Tatler*.[2]

It is hard to imagine that any one person could contemplate all these projects, not one by one over a series of years, but virtually all at once. On a number of them, to be sure, Percy had made considerable progress before he actually came to an agreement with the publisher. But it is doubtful that his work on any of them goes back further than 1758, and for some—the edition of Surrey's poems, for example—the signing of the agreement was the signal for Percy to begin work in earnest.

I   The Chinese Books

On February 28, 1758, Percy borrowed from Captain James Wilkinson of Bugbrooke in Northamptonshire "The History of Shuey Ping Sin, a Chinese Novel in 4 books, MS. Stitch'd in blue Paper," along with the argument of a Chinese play in two loose sheets of paper, and "Four Chinese Books, with Cutts."[3] The four Chinese books appear to have been the Chinese original of *Hau Kiou Choaan,* of which "The History of Shuey Ping Sin" was a translation, with three of its parts in English and the fourth in Portugese. Thus it was that Percy, who did not know Chinese but had learned Portugese in order to read Camoens,[4] set about preparing a translation of a Chinese novel for publication.

The English manuscript translation, which was dated 1719, was the work of James Wilkinson, an uncle of the Captain Wilkinson from whom Percy borrowed the manuscript. A representative of the East India Company who had spent many years in Canton, Wilkinson had apparently translated the novel to help himself learn Chinese. Just who translated the last section of the novel is not known; Ch'ên Shou-Yi suggests that Wilkinson probably studied Chinese at Macao either under a Portugese tutor or with a Portugese student under a Chinese tutor, and it may be that the Portugese translation was the work of a Portugese tutor or fellow student.[5]

On February 5, 1759, Percy finished the first book of *Hau Kiou Choaan,* and on February 13 he began writing the second. On February 19, having heard from Grainger that Dodsley "thinks well of the Novel," Percy set off for London, where on February 26 he read part of the novel to Dodsley and spent the evening with Dodsley and Goldsmith. On March 8 he and Dodsley reached an agreement to publish. He sent his first copy to Dodsley on August 5, 1759, and the book was published on November 14, 1761, in four small volumes.[6] In its final form, it included not only *Hau Kiou Choaan* but also "A Collection of Chinese Proverbs and Apothegms," which was intruded between parts of the novel at the end of volume three; the "Argument of a Chinese Play"; "A Dissertation on the Poetry of the Chinese" extracted from Fréret's *L'Histoire de l'Academie Royale;* and "Fragments of Chinese Poetry," translated by Percy from French translations. These last were placed at the end of volume 4, and each volume had as its frontspiece a line drawing taken from the original and illustrating a scene from the novel.

Hau Kiou Choaan, which had been published anonymously in China about 1660, is the story of the seventeen-year-old Shuey-ping-sin, left alone in her house because her father has been sent into exile, and of her admirer and protector, the student Tieh-chung-u. Shuey-ping-sin, "exquisitely beautiful" but "no less distinguished for the rare endowments of her mind" (I, 69–70), is pursued by the ruthless Kwo-khé-tzu, who is abetted by her wicked uncle Shuey-guwin. She manages to outwit her oppressor, however, by tricking him into marrying her ugly cousin in the belief that he is marrying Shuey-ping-sin, and through a series of quick-witted maneuvers she foils his subsequent efforts to force himself upon her. When it seems that the inexhaustible Kwo-khe-tzu will at last have his way, Tieh-chung-u, himself beset at times by Shuey-ping-sin's enemies, comes to her assistance, her father is found to have been wrongfully banished, and the two young people are married and their enemies punished. "I should not intreat your LADYSHIP's acceptance of the following sheets," wrote Percy in his dedication to the countess of Sussex, "... if they were not designed to countenance virtue and to discourage vice" (I, v).

Although in his preface he praised the novel for its morality, for its unity of design, and for its having "less of the marvellous and more of the probable" (I, xiv) than most Eastern compositions, it is evident that Percy found the account of Shuey-ping-sin's adventures less interesting for its narrative than for its glimpses into the Chinese character and customs. The "Editor," as he called himself, thus presented the novel "not as a piece to be admired for the beauties of its composition, but as a curious specimen of Chinese literature ... [and] as a faithful picture of Chinese manners, wherein the domestic and political oeconomy of that vast people is displayed with an exactness and accuracy to which none but a native could be capable of attaining" (I, xiv–xv). With characteristic thoroughness, he set about illuminating the unfamiliar ways of an unfamiliar people, and he made up for his own want of experience by a resourceful use of the 1738 translation of Pierre du Halde's *Description of the Empire of China and of Chinese Tartary* and twenty-five other works on the Orient. If *Hau Kiou Choaan* was the first Chinese novel to be printed in England, it was probably also the first novel of any kind to be so conscientiously edited. Its scholarly apparatus included not merely a preface but innumerable annotations, a bibliography, and even a fifteen-page index. Percy's notes, ranging in length from short sentences to essays of several hundred words, are almost always lucid, informative, and interesting, so that if Percy had not constantly cited his authorities the reader might readily have been deceived into thinking himself in the company of an experienced traveler:

If the *Chinese* are not disposed to see company, it is sufficient to say, that they are not at home: in which case if the visitant leaves his *paper of compliments* ... with the porter or servant, the visit is the same as if received in person, and must be returned in form. Sometimes a Mandarine will receive the *billet* by his porter, and will send to desire the visitant not to be at the trouble to alight from his chair. In either case the visit must be returned, either the same day, or on one of the three following, and if possible in the morning.

If a person is desirous of being excused the trouble of receiving these civilities, he affixes over his gate a paper written with white letters, "That he is retired to his garden house." (III, 61–62)

Enthusiastic as he was about his task, Percy never became a wholehearted admirer of the Chinese. His book reflects the conflicting attitudes of the Jesuit missionaries and the merchant adventurers, both of whom were represented in his bibliography, for it is laudatory and condemnatory by turns, sometimes even in the same sentence: "As the *Chinese* are distinguished for filial piety beyond all other nations, so they seem to carry this to an idolatrous excess" (I, 163). Percy's index, which refers largely to his own notes, provides a virtual catalog of Chinese traits of character as Percy saw them, and it can hardly be said that the admirable qualities predominate. The index begins with the "AFFECTATION of the *Chinese*," and under the heading "CHINESE" one finds fourteen entries for "*The dark side of their character*," including "cheats, the greatest in the world," "crafty," "corrupt," and "cowardly." The twelve for "*The bright side of their character*" include "ingenious," "industrious," "modest," and "studious" —none of them a sufficient counterpoise for the greatest cheats in the world.

Percy's editorial enthusiasm was to some degree a handicap, since it limited his ability for appropriate self-restraint. His mind overflowed with facts and comments, and he worked too quickly and with altogether too much impatience to set down what he knew. The result was that numerous pages in the book were canceled, three of the four volumes contain several pages each of "Additions and Corrections," and three contain substantial lists of "Errata." Even the 75-page "Collection of Chinese Proverbs and Apothegms" at the end of volume 3 was followed immediately by sections entitled "Proverbs Omitted," "Proverbs Corrected," and "Parallels Omitted." Dodsley's harried printer could not have been happy to learn in May, 1761, when Percy and Dodsley came to their series of agreements, that five more of Percy's works were being readied for the press.

The book had other faults, too, as several commentators familiar with the Chinese original have pointed out. Some of them are traceable, of course, to James Wilkinson, who had only a beginner's knowledge of Chinese and who was sometimes misled by the old Chinese practice of printing books with no punctuation and few paragraph divisions. In Percy's work, wrote T. C. Fan, "Paragraphs run together; sentences run together; and dialogues become statements and statements become dialogues."[7] John Francis Davis, in the preface to his 1829 translation of the novel, called the Percy edition "little better than a copious abstract," since much of the original was omitted, including almost all its poetical passages, and much was mistranslated or interpolated. Yet, concluded Davis,

it would be absurd to detract from the merit of Dr. Percy's labours on account of the imperfection of his materials, or to deny that he most ably edited, and very correctly illustrated (except where his version misled him) what certainly was, at the time when it appeared, by far the best picture of Chinese manners and society that we possessed.[8]

Percy's *Hau Kiou Choaan* appeared just after the decade when, as William Appleton observes, the cult of *Chinoiserie* had reached its height in England.[9] Colorful and even exciting as it often was, the cult was essentially a superficial one, with its attention centered largely on the quaint, the unusual, and the picturesque— on gardens, on pavilions like Sir William Chambers's pagoda at Kew, and on such useful and attractive articles as textiles, porcelain, wallpaper, and furniture. Thus it is not surprising that, even though the cult can be traced back to the middle of the seventeenth century, no English scholar had concentrated upon a work of Chinese literature with anything approaching the intensity of Percy's interest in *Hau Kiou Choaan*. The British were so ignorant of Chinese literature, in fact, that the very authenticity of *Hau Kiou Choaan* was questioned, with the result that Percy felt it necessary, when the second edition of the *Reliques* was published in 1767, to conclude the third volume with an extract of a letter from Canton to James Garland asserting that the novel existed and was known at Canton. In 1774, to allay any further doubts, he inserted an advertisement in the remaining copies of *Hau Kiou Choaan* identifying James Wilkinson as the translator for the first time, although he continued to preserve his own anonymity as "Editor." Even as late as 1802 he seems to have found it desirable to confirm the novel's authenticity, for, tipped into the first volume of his own copy of the *Miscellaneous Pieces Relating to the Chinese,* is a letter from George Thomas Staunton dated December 14, 1802, and stating that Staunton has checked in China on the original of *Hau Kiou Choaan* and is glad to report the success of his inquiry.[10]

The proverbs, poems, and argument of a play inserted in *Hau Kiou Choaan* would have fitted better into the *Miscellaneous Pieces Relating to the Chinese,* which was published in two volumes on December 13, 1762, only a little more than a year after the novel's four volumes.[11] The *Miscellaneous Pieces* consisted of seven selections which Percy had doubtless noted with interest while he was editing *Hau Kiou Choaan,* and he introduced them with a short preface and a "Dissertation on the Language and Characters of the Chinese." The selections include four pieces translated by Percy from the French, most notably the Chinese play *The Little Orphan of the House of Chao,* which Arthur Murphy had adapted for the English stage in 1759 under the title *The Orphan of China*; a 1750 English translation of the German J. L. de Mosheim's *Authentic Memoirs of the Christian Church in China*; Richard Hurd's "On the Chinese Drama"; and William Chambers's "Of the Art of Laying out Gardens among the Chinese." There are signs of editorial haste in the page of "Corrigenda" at the end of volume 2, in Percy's failure to secure Richard Hurd's permission to reprint his essay until after the book was published,[12] and in his proceeding to translate Frère Attiret's "Description of the Emperor of China's Garden and Pleasure-Houses near Peking" only to discover that a translation of much of the description had been published in 1752 (I, 147). But editorially the book is much less untidy than *Hau Kiou Choaan,* for by and large Percy simply let the authors speak for themselves. There are comparatively few footnotes and no notes are tucked in at the end. By the same token, it is the less interesting of the two books.

The preface is notable for little else than an eccentric Percy judgment. Like a number of his contemporaries, Percy was excited by the "discovery" made by Turberville Needham, an English Jesuit living in Italy, that the Chinese characters had been derived from Egyptian hieroglyphics, and the demonstration of Needham's error did not come until 1764, too late for Percy to revise his preface. Percy's "Dissertation on the Language and Characters of the Chinese," on the other hand, has no such besetting fault: it is, in fact, a work of considerable substance. As Vincent Ogburn pointed out,[13] it appears to be Percy's response to the suggestion of a "prefatory discourse upon the manner of writing in China" put forward by Ralph Griffiths when he was considering publishing *Hau Kiou Choaan,* and it brought together, in Percy's typically lucid and persuasive way, just about all that was known of the Chinese written language in 1762. In discussing the difficulty of a written language of some 80,000 characters, Percy portrays the Chinese attitude toward literary merit in striking terms which help appreciably to adjust the darker picture of the Chinese people which emerges from *Hau Kiou Choaan*:

If the difficulty of mastering and retaining such a number of arbitrary marks, greatly retards the progress of their literature; on the other hand the *Chinese* have all possible inducements to cultivate and pursue it. There is no part of the globe where learning is attended with such honours and rewards: the *Literati* are reverenced as men of another species, they are the only nobility known in *China*: be their birth never so mean and low, they become Mandarines of the highest rank in proportion to the extent of their learning: on the other hand be their birth never so exalted, they quickly sink into poverty and obscurity, if they neglect those studies which raised their fathers. It is a fond and groundless action of some late writers, who ought to have known better, that there is a key to the *Chinese* characters, hidden from the common people, and reserved as a secret in some few families of the great. On the contrary, there is no nation in the world where the first honours of the state lie so open to the lowest of the people, and where there is less of hereditary and traditional greatness. All the state employments in *China* are the rewards of literary merit: and they are continually grasped by hands lifted up from among the common people. (I, 20–21)

For the "late writers, who ought to have known better," Percy referred his readers to volume 8 of the *Modern Universal History,* which had been published in 1760. During the editing of *Hau Kiou Choaan* and the *Miscellaneous Pieces,* Percy prepared "Remarks on the History of China" in the "Modern Part" of the *Universal History,* an essay which exists in two manuscripts in the Huntington Library.[14] The longer and apparently the later of these contains a trenchant analysis of the *Universal History* writer's ignorance of Spanish and Portugese and of China and the Chinese, and there is no reason why it should not have been acceptable to one or more periodical editors of Percy's day. Its not being published is accounted for in a Percy note appended to the manuscript many years later: "NB. I had once thought of publishing a Pamphlet to correct the Mistakes of that Volume &c but being informed afterwards that poor old Psalmanazar was the compiler of that Part of the Universal History I laid aside my Intention on account of the Age & Poverty of the Author."[15] George Psalmanazar, the brilliant impostor who had once taught Britons a "Formosan" language he had himself invented, had died in May, 1763, at the age of about eighty-four, a revered and apparently a contrite man. Even Johnson, who "reverenced him for his piety," would not oppose him: "I should as soon think of contradicting a BISHOP," he said.[16] It would not be surprising if Percy learned of Psalmanazar's authorship from Johnson, who in 1784 provided John Nichols with the names of *Universal History* contributors,[17] or if in Johnson's company he himself acquired a reverence for Psalmanazar's piety as well as for his age and poverty.

II The Matrons

A work suited to the *Miscellaneous Pieces Related to the Chinese* was probably the inspiration for *The Matrons,* which Dodsley published anonymously on May 28, 1762.[18] In the story of the Chinese matron, adapted by Percy from Du Halde, the Lady Tien reacts with indignation upon hearing of a young widow who fanned the grave of her dead husband because he had implored her not to remarry until the wet earth on his tomb was dry; yet Lady Tien is herself quickly betrothed to a young student when she presumes her own husband to be dead. Oliver Goldsmith had made use of the story in the series of Chinese letters printed in the *Public Ledger* in 1760 and 1761 and collected in 1762 under the title *The Citizen of the World*. In letter XVIII, which appeared on March 15, 1760, Lien Chi Altangi cites Lady Tien's perfidy to underscore the dangers of romantic marriages for the edification of a merchant friend in Amsterdam. Percy, who had recently married the "Nancy" of his choice, had no such objective. He perceived the story as exemplifying the familiar theme of the frailty of widows, and, as Cleanth Brooks has noted, it must have reminded him immediately of Petronius's classic tale of *The Ephesian Matron*.[19] As one who had an abiding interest in comparative cultures and literatures, he would surely have been pleased that two cultures so different as the Chinese and the Roman could produce stories so similar in theme.

The initial agreement with Dodsley called for three stories. What the third story was that Percy had at hand in May, 1761, is not known, but a likely choice is *The French Matron*, which he would have found among the works of Buckingham that he was soon to begin reediting for Jacob Tonson.[20] In its final form *The Matrons*, in addition to the three stories already mentioned, contained *The British Matron*, from Benjamin Victor's *The Widow of the Wood* (1755); *The Turkish Matron*, from George Lyttleton's *The Court Secret* (1741); and *The Roman Matron*, from a black-letter adaptation of *The Ephesian Matron* entitled *The Seven Wise Maisters of Rome*. Even with its six stories *The Matrons* forms a not very substantial duodecimo. As originally projected it would have been a very slender volume indeed.

As for the work itself, little of it beyond the choice of stories and the translations of two of them can be called Percy's own. A note at the end of the page of "Contents" states that "The two first are new Translations"; and although T. C. Fan has expressed the view that the story of the Chinese matron was adapted from the English translation of Du Halde's *A Description of China* published by Edward Cave in 1738–1741, Percy's version seems sufficiently different to justify his claim of originality. His other writing in the volume seems to have been confined to the dedication, the translation of *The Ephesian*

Matron, and the brief introductions to the stories of the British and Roman matrons.[21]

Of these, the "Dedication to the Matrons of Great Britain and Ireland" merits some slight attention. Written with elegance and spirit, it assures Percy's feminine readers that, even though the six stories may be thought to bear hard upon them, they do in effect constitute a panegyric, since to gather them together it has been necessary "to ransack the mouldy volumes of Antiquity, and to take a voyage as far as China." But, he adds, even the "richest diamond-mine does not contain all true brilliants," and the more we condemn the "levity or wantonness" of those widows whose weeds merely cloak their immodesty, the more we must admire the virtue of others. Thus his book does not result from "the warm resentment of some disappointed lover" or "the accumulated spleen of some surly old bachelor"; it comes from one with the interest of the sex so much at heart "that he wishes no individual of it ever to act amiss" (ii–iv).

Concluding as it did with the decapitation of the Roman matron, the book's moral. thrust can be said to have required little articulation. If anything, it was in need of the softening that Percy attempted to give it in his dedication. The reviewer for the *Monthly Review* seems to have thought so too: "A notable compendium this! admirably well calculated to encourage matrimony!... yet let... [the fair sex] not be discouraged: for ... the instances are truly singular; one of a nation."[22]

III   *The Scandinavian Literature*

Percy's interest in Scandinavian literature and history, if not aroused, was certainly encouraged by his Northamptonshire neighbor Edward Lye, rector of the nearby church at Yardley Hastings. As Percy noted in a memorial he prepared for the use of Owen Manning after Lye's death in 1767, Lye—"one of the first Grammarians of his Age"—understood French, Italian, Swedish, and Danish and had become eminent for his knowledge of Anglo-Saxon and "all the Northern Tongues."[23] He had published editions of Junius's *Etymologicum Anglicanum* in 1743 and the Gothic Gospels in 1750, and at the time of his death had almost completed an Anglo-Saxon dictionary, which Manning carried through to publication. In recording that he had himself learned the runic letters on February 3, 1759, Percy expressed the view that they were probably as familiar to Lye as his Pater Noster.[24]

When Percy contracted with Dodsley for *Five Pieces of Runic Poetry* on May 21, 1761, the book was probably just about ready for publication. He had informed William Shenstone of his project in a letter of September, 1760, and had been advised by Shenstone to include only brief notes and a short preface and to translate the poems in "a kind of *flowing* yet *pompous* Prose."[25] His translation of "The Incantation of Hervor" was published in the *Lady's Magazine* for June, 1761,[26] and on July 21 he asserted confidently to Evan Evans that the book would make its appearance during the winter.[27] Publication was delayed, however, until April 2, 1763, by what Percy, in a prefatory note, chose to call simply an "accident."[28]

For his information about the Icelandic language and customs, Percy relied heavily on Lye, who compared the versions used by Percy with the originals, and upon Henri Mallet's *L'Introduction à l'Histoire de Dannemarc*, which Percy was soon to begin translating. Only two of the pieces, "The Dying Ode of Regner Lodbrog" and "The Ransome of Egill the Scald," were taken directly from the Icelandic originals, although all five of the Icelandic texts were printed at the end of the volume. "The Incantation of Hervor," as Percy noted, was taken from the translation of George Hickes "with some considerable emendations," and "The Funeral Song of Hacon" and "The Complaint of Harold" were derived chiefly from Latin versions (4, 61, 74–75). Percy's practice was criticized by William Herbert in his *Select Icelandic Poetry*, published in 1804, and by Walter Scott when he reviewed Herbert's *Miscellaneous Poetry* two years later. Herbert argued, with obvious justice, that translations filtered through a Latin medium could not be expected to represent the style and spirit of the originals;[29] and Scott singled out specific poems for attention, among them "The Complaint of Harold," in which Percy failed to see that Harold was rewarded with the Russian maiden's hand and thus turned a love song into a complaint.[30]

Although Percy had learned the runic characters, he could

hardly be said to have felt at home in the Icelandic language, and it is not surprising that his translations—in the *"flowing yet pompous"* prose that Shenstone had urged—failed to capture the joy and tumult of battle or the clash of sword and buckler that reverberates through the poems:

We fought with swords, at Bardafyrda. A shower of blood rained from our weapons. Headlong fell the palid corpse a prey for the hawks. The bow gave a twanging sound. The blade sharply bit the coats of mail: it bit the helmet in the fight. The arrow sharp with poison and all besprinkled with bloody sweat ran to the wound. ("The Dying Ode of Regner Lodbrog," p. 33)

Aware of his limitations, Percy did not proffer his work as a model of poetic translation, although he was not prepared to relinquish all claims to success. "I humbly conceive," he wrote to Dr. Robert Anderson on August 16, 1804, after Anderson had informed him of Herbert's comments in *Select Icelandic Poetry,* "an English reader will form thereby as good a notion of the peculiar images and general subject of the original, as from . . . [Herbert's] own paraphrase . . . in English verse."[31]

Percy's inspiration for *Five Pieces of Runic Poetry,* as acknowledged in his preface, was the success of the Erse fragments published by James Macpherson in June, 1760, but he confessed that it was by no means in the interest of his "little work" to have it compared with the "beautiful" Erse pieces. And yet, he added, with a skepticism that probably reflected his conversations with Samuel Johnson, until the translator thinks it proper to produce the originals, it is impossible to say whether the Erse fragments "do not owe their superiority, if not their whole existence" to him. As editor of the runic pieces, he himself had "no such boundless field for licence": every poem had already been published with a Latin or Swedish version and every deviation was therefore readily detectable ([vi–vii]).

Percy's real purpose, in short, was a scholarly one. His interest in the early literature of his own and other countries was profound, and at this time of his life it came close to being all-consuming. Writing to Evan Evans on August 14, 1762, he expressed the wish that Evans might follow his *Five Pieces of*

Runic Poetry with a "Collection of British Poetry," and then all the pamphlets of early poetry could be thrown together in one volume with a title such as *Specimens of the Ancient Poetry of Different Nations*:

I have for some time had a project of this kind, and with a view to it am exciting several of my friends to contribute their share. Such a work might fill up two neat pocket volumes. Besides the *Erse Poetry*: the *Runic Poetry*: and some *Chinese Poetry* that was published last winter at the end of a book called *Hau Kiou choaan* or *The Pleasing History* 4 vol. Besides these, I have procured a MS. translation of the celebrated *Tograi Carmen* from the Arabic: and have set a friend to translate *Solomon's Song* afresh from the Hebrew, chiefly with a view to the poetry; this also is printing off and will soon be published in a shilling pamphlet. Then I have myself gleaned up specimens of *East-Indian Poetry*: *Peruvian Poetry*: *Lapland Poetry*: *Greenland Poetry*: and inclosed I send you one specimen of *Saxon Poetry*.[32]

Whether or not one volume, or two neat pocket volumes, could have contained it, not surprisingly even the indefatigable Percy never brought this ambitious project to completion. He went a good way with it, however, and it is doubtful that anyone else in his time could have contributed so much toward it himself and at the same time stimulated others, as Percy stimulated Evan Evans, to join him in it. For Percy had not only a broad knowledge and a boundless curiosity; his enthusiasm was almost instantaneously infectious. His curiosity, moreover, was never content with trifles. The misfortune of the Icelandic poets, he wrote in his preface, is that "their compositions have fallen into the hands of none but professed antiquarians: and these have only selected such poems for publication as confirmed some fact in history, or served to throw light on the antiquities of their country" ([xi]). Percy, of course, had no contempt for either historical fact or the illumination of antiquities. But his pervasive interest was the character, manners, and cultures of early societies as these were reflected in their literature: all five of his runic pieces, he noted, demonstrate that poetry was once held "in the highest estimation" by the people of the North ([iii]). More than anything else, it was this humanist quality of Percy's work that justified Johnson's tribute to him for giving "grace and splendour to his studies of antiquity."

If Percy's runic translations do not convey the excitement of their originals, they nonetheless merit attention as the first serious attempt in Britain to encourage interest in the neglected Norse poetry by making it understandable to his generation and seeing it in relationship to other literatures. With *Five Pieces of Runic Poetry*, as with *Hau Kiou Choaan*, Percy's peculiar blend of curiosity, learning, and energy carried him to frontiers where he was well in advance of his contemporaries and where he could mark the riches accessible to those who might follow. The influence of Percy's work is suggested, as Margaret Omberg pointed out, by the fact that the majority of Nordic translations in the late eighteenth cenury were new versions of Percy's five pieces: fourteen of "The Dying Ode of Regner Lodbrog," for example, and eight each of "The Incantation of Hervor" and "The Complaint of Harold."[33]

Even for Percy *Five Pieces of Runic Poetry* did not mark the end of his quest. Less reluctant to trumpet his works than to disclose his identity—his name appeared in none of his books until the *Reliques* was published in 1765—he announced in the preface that a translation of Paul Henri Mallet's *L'Introduction à l'Histoire de Dannemarc* was "in great forwardness" ([x]). Those words may have described the state of the translation in Percy's mind or of his negotiations with the booksellers. He had, to be sure, attempted to interest the publisher Andrew Millar in a translation as early as December, 1762, and he was assured of publication by John Newbery in June, 1763.[34] But as an indication of actual progress they were at best misleading, for, as Percy noted in his diary, he did not begin the translation until November 21, 1763, more than seven months after informing the public that it was "in great forwardness."

Mallet's book, written in French, had been published in Copenhagen in two volumes in 1755 and 1756, with a second edition appearing at Geneva in 1763, and Percy seems himself to have projected a two-volume translation from the time of his initial interest in the project. Formidable though his task was—it included a translation of the *Prose Edda* from Mallet's French[35]—Percy worked at it steadily and at times with great rapidity. On

May 17, 1764, he translated twenty-two pages, wrote ten letters, and took two rides, accomplishments which required that he stay up from four in the morning until midnight. On July 24 and 26 of that year he read parts of his translation to Samuel Johnson and Mrs. Williams, who were spending much of the summer with the Percys in Easton Mauduit.[36] The first volume, minus the preface, was in print by the summer of 1765, and on February 7, 1767, Percy noted that he spent the day preparing the second volume for the press.[37] "My version of Mallet," he wrote Evans a few weeks later on March 1, "has been long suspended, but is now drawing towards a speedy Conclusion and I hope will be published this Spring."[38] He was so optimistic about publication, in fact, that in the second edition of the *Reliques,* published on December 3, 1767,[39] he actually cited the book in a note as though it were already available to the public: "See al[s]o 'A Description of the Manners, Customs, &c. of the ancient Danes and other northern nations: from the French of M. Mallet' 2 vol. 8vo" (I, xx). Percy's use of the book's subtitle suggests that the title *Northern Antiquities* was an afterthought, perhaps one of the few compensations for the long wait until the book finally made its appearance on June 8, 1770.[40]

Unquestionably Percy found a kindred spirit in Mallet. For both men the ancient literatures unlocked many of the most coveted secrets of the past. Why "should history be only a recital of battles, sieges, intrigues and negotiations?" Mallet asks in Percy's translation. "And why should it contain meerly a heap of petty facts and dates, rather than a just picture of the opinions, customs and even inclinations of a people?" (I, 55). The most credulous writer, Mallet continues,

he that has the greatest passion for the marvelous, while he falsifies the history of his contemporaries, paints their manners of life and modes of thinking, without perceiving it. His simplicity, his ignorance, are at once pledges of the artless truth of his drawing, and a warning to distrust that of his relations. This is doubtless the best, if not the only use, we can make of those old reliques of poetry, which have escaped the shipwreck of time. (I, 56)

Percy might well have used the passage as an epigraph for the most ancient pieces in the *Reliques.*

Mallet, with Percy at his heels, leads one through the old literature into examinations of the religion of Odin, the ancient forms of government, the Scandinavian passion for war, and the restless exploration and conquest of Britain and Northern Europe. Only at one point does Percy dissociate himself from his writer, and his disagreement on that point was of such significance that he made it the subject of his preface to the two volumes and returned to it frequently in his notes to the text. Mallet's error, as Percy described it, was in "supposing the ancient Gauls and Germans, the Britons and Saxons, to have been all originally one and the same people; thus confounding the antiquities of the Gothic and Celtic nations" (I, ii). Supported by Evan Evans, whom he consulted through their correspondence, Percy found evidence for the distinction between the two peoples in their physical appearances, their manners and customs, their institutions and laws, and above all their religion and language. These last two, he asserted, are "so strong and conclusive, that the whole proof might be left to rest upon them" (I, xiii).

Writing long before the discoveries of nineteenth-century philologists, Percy was led to conclude that the Gothic and Celtic languages were so "radically and essentially different" that they could not have been derived from a common source (I, xx). It is not surprising therefore that I. A. Blackwell, in the Bohn edition of *Northern Antiquities* published in 1847, devoted a good many pages to demonstrating the common roots of Gothic and Celtic in the Indo-European family of languages, with which Percy was not familiar.[41] Percy, to be sure, was by no means a thoroughly reliable guide. But exploration of the unknown or the little known was his passion, and, as with all explorers striding out along new paths, it was inevitable that he would occasionally become entangled in the briars or mistake a thicket for a wood. More remarkable was that, unschooled as he was, he could bring to the study of northern antiquities a mind capable of adjusting even the extraordinary learning of a scholar like Mallet. For his own countrymen, Percy opened up vistas which excited scholars like Evan Evans and inspired poets like William Blake, whose imaginative use of the Gothic mythology helped to change the course of English poetry.[42] Percy's sights may have been set beyond his reach, but in keeping them fixed on the horizon he traveled further along unfamiliar roads than anyone but himself could probably have dreamed of.[43]

IV   *The Religious Works*

No one has asserted a claim for Percy as an eminent theologian or biblical scholar. His religious works, including his published sermons, are few, and to one of them he was attracted in much the same way that he was attracted to the poetry of China and Scandinavia: it was one of the "specimens of the ancient poetry of different nations." *The Song of Solomon,* as we have seen, was contracted for with Robert Dodsley on the same day as *Five Pieces of Runic Poetry,* and when it was published four years later Percy made certain to define its purpose in the very first line of his preface. His edition was "an attempt to rescue one of the most beautiful pastorals in the world, as well as the most ancient," from the "obscurity and confusion" resulting from "the injudicious practice of former commentators," who by and large had been so busy unfolding its "allegorical meaning" that they had totally neglected its "literal sense" (v).

Percy had more evident qualifications for this task than for editing *Hau Kiou Choaan* or translating Icelandic verse. As an Oxford master of arts and an ordained minister, he was thoroughly schooled in the Bible, and at Oxford he had entered conscientiously into the study of Hebrew under the Polish immigrant Mark Moses Vowel. Among his earliest essays were the Hebrew criticisms and dissertations which he offered to Ralph Griffiths in 1761 for publication in *The Library.* He was able, in addition, to call upon the Reverend Robert Binnel of Newport, Shropshire, who supplied comments upon the text and more than a dozen extended notes before his death on April 26, 1763. Binnel's death was an obvious blow to Percy, who eulogized his friend warmly at the end of his preface to *The Song of Solomon* (ix–x).

For Percy, *The Song of Solomon* was neither the unified drama in the classical mold that some critics had found it nor a series of distinct eclogues bearing "no more relation to each other, than so many pastorals of Virgil or Theocritus" (xiii). Following the lead of the French critic Bossuet, he divided *The Song of Solomon* into seven parts representing the seven days of a "nuptial solemnity," and within the framework of this "dramatic eclogue" he assigned each verse to a designated speaker: the bridegroom, the spouse, the companions of the bridegroom, or the virgins attending the spouse.

So various were the interpretations of *The Song of Solomon* that Percy found it desirable to support his own interpretation with a commentary in seven parts, one for each of the seven days' eclogues, and to append to the translation some fifty pages of notes upon the text. After the book had gone to press, a new edition of Bishop Lowth's *Praelectiones* was published with notes by Professor J. D. Michaelis of the University of Göttingen attacking the view that *The Song of Solomon* is a nuptial poem, and Percy took the opportunity to defend his opinion still further in a five-page "Postscript."

Percy's book was published anonymously on June 13, 1764,[44] and its editor was praised in the June *St. James's Magazine* for his ingenuity and critical knowledge and in the July *Critical Review* for his taste and learning and for the quality of his translation.[45] Inevitably the translation owed much to the King James version. Numerous verses—"Many waters cannot quench love," for example—were left untouched, and others were only slightly altered.[46] Perhaps Percy's most serious problems arose out of his attempt to find coherent dramatic sequence in the poem and to assign each verse to one or another of the speakers. The anonymous author of *The Song of Solomon Paraphrased*, published in 1775 and directed largely at Percy's translation, charged Percy with relying too heavily upon the customs of modern Jews, Arabs, and other Eastern peoples and thus being misled, for example, into the "indelicacy" of supposing that Solomon would permit his bride to be chastised by the watchmen. He attributed to the same cause the "indecent supposition" that the bridegroom's companions would actually witness the consummation of the marriage, but this seems rather to have been an ambiguity arising out of the lack of stage directions in Percy's biblical text.[47]

If the book were approved, Percy wrote in his preface, he would inquire in some future work into the sublime truths hidden beneath *The Song of Solomon's* "literal sense" (vi). Whether he felt that the book was not sufficiently approved—it was not re-printed—or was simply deterred by the weight of other responsibilities, he never carried out his intention. Characteristically, however, he compiled a collection of translations of *The Song of Solomon* containing forty-one printed volumes and two manuscripts, and he presented it to the Lambeth Palace Library in April, 1782, shortly after he was appointed bishop of Dromore.[48]

A more popular religious work was *A Key to the New Testament*, the idea for which may have come to Percy as early as 1761, when he made the acquaintance of the book's publisher, Lockyer Davis. Of his two major sources, the English translation of J. D. Michaelis's *Introductory Lectures to the Sacred Books of the New Testament* was published in that year, and Nathaniel Lardner's *History of the Apostles and Evangelists, Writers of the New Testament, with Remarks and Observations on Every Book* was published in 1760. The actual writing of the book many not have begun until 1764, when still another useful source, Henry Owen's *Observations on the Four Gospels,* made its appearance. By August of that year, when Johnson was visiting the Percys at Easton Mauduit, Percy was correcting a proof sheet, probably of his introduction, and "preparing Copy of St. Matthews Gospel," and it is probable therefore that both those sections of the book derived some benefit from Percy's discussions with his guest.[49]

Percy's purpose, as he announced in his preface, was to provide a clear "introductory illustration" of the books of the New Testament, showing "the design of their writers, the nature of their contents, and whatever else is previously necessary to their being read with understanding" (v). A well executed work of this kind, he noted, would prove the best commentary and frequently preclude the want of any other, since "it directs the Reader right at his first setting out, and thereby saves him the trouble of much after-inquiry."

When he made George Paton a present of the *Key* on June 12, 1769, Percy informed Paton that he had printed the book for the use of his parishioners.[50] It is an engaging thought—Percy and his London printer laboring at pen and press for his tiny flocks at Wilby and Easton Mauduit—but it must be set down as a characteristic Percy belittling of his own efforts. No doubt Percy developed some of his ideas for his weekly appearances at his two parish churches, but the book was obviously intended for a wider audience, and it found it. One or another of its half dozen editions between 1766 and 1806 was probably consulted by most English clergymen of that period and by students preparing for holy orders at the universities, for it set forth concisely and lucidly much of what they needed to know about the New Testament. Percy's materials, to be sure, were available elsewhere; his contribution was to bring them together in a convenient pocket-sized volume which could be purchased for the modest price of two shillings.

In addition to Percy's short preface, the volume's introductory material includes an account of the sects and heresies at the time of Christ which had been sent to Percy by an unidentified "ingenious friend." The same friend supplied the "Key to the Prophecies Contained in the Revelation" which concludes the volume (ix–x). Percy's introduction contains elementary information which even the most humble among his Wilby and Easton Mauduit congregations could have had no difficulty comprehending—"The holy Scriptures are divided into The OLD and NEW TESTAMENT"—but it quickly turns to more abstruse definition and closes with a brief discussion of the chronological order of the gospels, much of it quoted from Owen's *Observations*. In his text Percy takes up each book of the New Testament successively and provides information on dates and authorship and often a section by section analysis varying in length from book to book. "Now we shall find St. John's Gospel divided into three Parts," he notes, and proceeds to enumerate them in three sentences (27). To St. John's three epistles he devotes barely two pages, but his analysis of the First Epistle to the Corinthians alone extends to three pages, and that of the Epistle to the Romans to seven. As biblical scholarship proliferated, the *Key* of course became outdated and was replaced. But it is a tribute to Percy's ability to sense and fill a need that the five editions of his lifetime, most of which he revised, were followed by further editions in the nineteenth century, when it was joined with Robert Gray's *Key to the Old Testament* in 1813 to form *A Key to the Holy Bible*. In that form it was republished in 1825 and 1842, but even as late as 1823 the *Key to the New Testament* was published separately at Cambridge.

Percy's only other religious publications were two charity sermons, but other sermons have survived in manuscript,[51] and the sermon that he preached at Oxford when he was awarded the doctor of divinity degree in July, 1793, has been described in the *Gentleman's Magazine*.[52] The manuscripts suggest that he seldom composed original sermons. Instead he adapted already published sermons or other moral works to his own uses and then preached his modified sermons again and again, with variations to suit particular occasions. He revised his friend Edward Blakeway's sermon on "The Christian Race and Conflict, Compared to Those of the Grecian Games" for delivery at Temple Church on January 17, 1768, and repeated it that year at Alnwick Church on August 28 and St. Leonard's, Bridgnorth on October 2. He preached it again at Carlisle Cathedral on September 23, 1781, at Dromore on April 30, 1786, and even before the king and queen at St. James's Chapel on December 10, 1775.[53]

Extensive though his modifications usually were, one of Percy's reworked sermons caused him considerable embarrassment. On May 11, 1769, he preached the annual charity "Sermon before the Sons of the Clergy" at St. Paul's Cathedral, when the offering was taken for the benefit of clergymen's widows and orphans. Choosing as his text John 13:35—"By this shall all men know that ye are my disciples, if ye have love one to another"—Percy found the "wonderful Superiority" of Christianity over other religions in its "promoting and inculcating the Duties of Beneficence" (1); and the stewards of the charity were sufficiently impressed to order the sermon's publication, as was their frequent but not inevitable practice. Percy's embarrassment on this occasion arose from the fact that, however freely, he had adapted the sermon from Johnson's *Idler* No. 4 without Johnson's knowledge, and he resisted publication vigorously until informed by the stewards that he had no choice.[54] Percy then asked Joseph Cradock to explain the circumstances to Johnson, who was "highly diverted" by Cradock's account and said with a laugh, "Pray, Sir, give my kind respects to Dr. Percy, and tell him, I desire he will do whatever he pleases in regard to my Idler; it is entirely at his service."[55]

Essentially Percy made use only of Johnson's central theme and its more general illustrations, both of which he developed in his own language and with much that was not in Johnson's essay. His other published charity sermon seems to have been entirely his own.[56] It was preached at Christ-Church, Dublin on April 18, 1790, before the Incorporated Society for Promoting English Protestant Schools in Ireland, and its text was taken from Proverbs 22:6: "Train up a child in the way he should go, and when he is old he will not depart from it." Having observed that "Men are chiefly distinguished from each other, by the advantages or want of Education" (3), Percy went on to praise those institutions that preserve young people from the evils of ignorance "by changing whole Nests of Rioters and Robbers into rising Nurseries of virtuous and useful Subjects!" (7). Ireland, he noted, had a particular problem. Though naturally "open, generous, and good-natured," the Irish are "quick in their Resentments", and having seen their ancestors forfeit their lands and inherited "deep Prejudices against the succeeding Proprietor," they are "too apt to consider his Stores and Possessions as lawful Plunder" and to oppose the laws which have secured the forfeiture that disinherited them (12–13). Illiteracy and ignorance have helped to perpetuate this unhappy state: "Too generally believing that Pilgrimages, Penances, Pecuniary Commutations, and External Observances can expiate Guilt, their poor untutored Minds are left open to the influence of every bad Passion, and evil Habit; and are unrestrained from the Commission of every Crime" (16).

By providing an education for the less fortunate, Percy contended, the English Protestant Charity Schools contributed to the security and safety of the more enlightened and to the happiness and welfare of the poor. The thirty-eight schools, he observed, admit children from the poorest Catholic families between the ages of six and ten, provide them an education in which labor and instruction are properly blended, apprentice them to Protestant families, and, provided they have certificates of good behavior at the end of their terms, give forty shillings to the boys and portions of five pounds to the girls that marry Protestants. No "Compulsion or undue Arts," said Percy, are used to gain these children because, in spite of their prejudices, their parents are too sensible of the advantages of this kind of education to wish to deny them to their children. In their fifty-six years, the schools had placed 6,647 children in agriculture, trade, or manufacture and given portions to 685 girls who married Protestants (17–18).

V   *The Northumberland Works*

For Percy the association with the Northumberland family was an extraordinarily happy one. From the time of his appointments as tutor to Algernon Percy in the spring of 1765 and chaplain to the earl of Northumberland on June 28 of that year, he was provided an apartment at Northumberland House in the Strand and invited to spend summers with the family at Alnwick Castle in Northumberland. In 1765 he left Easton Mauduit for Alnwick on July 17 and remained until October 16, a visit lengthened by a six-week tour of the Lake District and Scotland which he undertook with the young Algernon. In 1766 he left for the North on July 4 and stayed until August 25, and most subsequent summer visits were about of that duration.[57]

Over the years Percy performed numerous services for the Northumberland family, most of them highly congenial to one of his clerical and literary bent. He preached at Alnwick Church and heard the prayers of family and servants at Alnwick Castle. He cataloged the books at Syon House, the Northumberland residence on the Thames at Brentford, and he seems to have contributed his poetic talents in behalf of a favorite charity.[58] He wrote letters for his patron, assisted when the elder son, Lord Warkworth, was running for office, prepared genealogies for the duke, duchess, and Lord Warkworth, and helped to entertain the duke's guests. At Alnwick he quickly became enamored of the castle and its surroundings, and he regularly accompanied castle visitors to Hulne Park and its crumbling thirteenth-century Carmelite abbey, to Alnmouth on the North Sea, and to Warkworth, where the ruins of another Percy castle and an ancient hermitage stirred the poet in him to probe the mystery of their connection.

Percy's diary entries reveal that within a week of his arrival at Alnwick on July 21, 1765, he had ridden with the earl and countess of Northumberland (they became duke and duchess in 1766) "to take a View of the Sea," had twice visited Hulne Abbey, had traveled with Algernon to Alnmouth, and had

climbed Brisley Hill in Hulne Park. On July 30 he climbed
Brisley Hill again, and on the thirty-first he accompanied Algernon to Warkworth Castle and the hermitage. On August 5, a
rainy day, he took advantage of the earl's absence to describe
the ride to Hulne Abbey in a letter to Edward Lye, which in
revised form was privately printed that fall as A Letter Describing
the Ride to Hulne Abbey from Alnwick in Northumberland.[59]
The nine-page pamphlet was probably given routinely to castle
visitors, who seem almost as routinely to have taken the six-mile
ride around Hulne Park under Percy's guidance. In eleven summers for which his pocket diaries have survived during the period
1765 to 1781, Percy recorded more than forty such excursions.

Percy's letter, like a proper travel guide, is both descriptive
and historical. Leaving the castle by "the great gate," the rider
descends a "steep romantic hill," crosses a rivulet, and then
ascends until he reaches the top of Brisley Hill (VIII, 152–53).
From there he proceeds along a winding route past a cave (a
"fine romantic solitude"), after which he winds round the edge
of a precipice presenting "a noble prospect" with a glimpse of
Hulne Abbey far below (VIII, 154). The abbey itself, founded
in 1240 by the crusader Ralph Fresborn in return for a release
granted him by the monks of Mt. Carmel, appeared most striking
to Percy for its tower erected in the fifteenth century by the
fourth earl of Northumberland. The tower, he noted, was a
refuge for the monks during the ravages of the Scottish invaders,
for "these rude men spared no places or persons however sacred,
but laid all waste with fire and sword" (VIII, 156).

Privately printed also was The Regulations and Establishment
of the Houshold of Henry Algernon Percy, from a manuscript
prepared by the fifth earl of Northumberland between 1512 and
1525. For reasons Percy was unable to explain, the manuscript
came into the possession of the Lords Dacre, but in mid-eigh-
teenth century it was returned to the earl of Northumberland,
who lent it to Percy in the spring of 1765 for his use in compiling
a history of the house of Northumberland.[60] In the printed
volume, which Percy edited, he followed the text of the manuscript "with all possible exactness" (xxv), although he compen-
sated at times for the want of periods by supplying capital letters
at the beginning of sentences, and he also employed the equals

sign, which was not in use in the early sixteenth century. He added thirty-seven pages of notes and a 22-page preface which he wrote during the last week of November, 1770,[61] and the printing of an edition of two hundred copies, which had actually begun in 1767, was completed in that year. Most of the copies were distributed to the duke's friends, but a number went to such Percy friends as Samuel Johnson, Richard Farmer, Lord Hailes, and John Hawkins, who had supplied an extensive note on early choral music.[62]

The manuscript records in detail the procedures for regulating the economy of the fifth earl's castles at Wresill and Lekinfield in Yorkshire. It begins by noting the allotment of £78 16s. 8d. for over 2,100 bushels of wheat annually (4), and concludes with an order to the "Clerke Comptroillour" to "have an Ey" daily to the slaughtering in order to make sure that the suet is "clynne taikynne owt withoute any Bribe" and is then weighed, brought into the storehouse, and delivered to the chandler (410). In between it stipulates sums for every provision from larks to swine, sets the wages of household employments, and outlines tables of organization for such groups as the chaplains and priests and the gentlemen and children of the chapel choir. These petty concerns, Percy concluded, were the natural consequence of the emergence from the barbarity of earlier times, as the nobility strove "to keep their turbulent followers in peace and order" ([ix]). He surmised also that a nobleman of the dark ages, retired to his castle without books, newspapers, correspondence, cards, or visits to fill up his leisure hours, would turn naturally to close regulation of his household if he happened to be a prudent man ([x]).

No doubt Percy was reading too much of himself into the fifth earl's situation; it seems likely that, in the absence of newspapers and cards, an enterprising sixteenth-century nobleman could have found other amusements than compiling an encyclopedia of household minutiae, whatever solace that activity might give to prudence. But in his general picture of the fifth earl's establishment, Percy drew his lines clearly and strikingly. He saw immediately the manuscript's value as a record of ancient manners. It left, for example, no room to question the view that the magnificence of the old nobility was almost identical with

that of the royal court. Both crown and nobleman had household
plans, offices, and councils, as well as similar reliances on the
priesthood; even the form and style of their warrants were the
same. Percy showed also how the manuscript could be used as
a guide to the value of money in the early sixteenth century, and,
with typical Percy pride, he concluded that, even though the
fifth earl spent only £1,000 annually on his household of 166
persons, his housekeeping was characterized by "plenty and
liberality" ([x]–xiii).

Once again in *The Northumberland Houshold Book* Percy was
taking the lead in English scholarship. Although similar manuscripts existed, none had yet been published, and his effort, encouraged and supported by the duke of Northumberland, piqued
the imaginations of fellow antiquarians. A number of them not
included in the original distribution lists requested copies, and
the Reverend John Pickford, in his life of Percy prefixed to *The
Percy Folio Manuscript*, cites ten such manuscripts published
between 1787 and 1844.[63] Percy's own publication was reprinted
in the *Antiquarian Repertory* in 1809 (IV, 9–344) and in separate
editions in 1827 and 1905.

Percy, of course, was interested in all the Northumberland
possessions past and present, but he was particularly fascinated
by one of them. His summer excursions to Warkworth Castle and
its nearby hermitage were less numerous than his rides round
Hulne Abbey because of the six or seven miles which separated
Alnwick and Warkworth. The duchess was herself a frequent
visitor to the hermitage, however, and she suggested that Percy
collect what he could of its history and commit it to writing.[64]
On August 5, 1767, he described the hermitage in a letter to the
bishop of Carlisle in much the same way that he had written
to Edward Lye about Hulne Abbey.[65] But this time, instead of
transforming his letter into a pamphlet, he produced his poem
The Hermit of Warkworth, which was published in London on
May 21, 1771. Described on the title page as "A Northumberland
Ballad. In Three Fits or Cantos," it was dedicated to the duchess
of Northumberland by means of a Spenserian sonnet, and it
included a preliminary "Advertisement" and a postscript with a
variety of information about the hermitage. Before publication,
Percy generously distributed sixty copies to his friends, including
the entire membership of the Club.[66]

Percy found the hermitage attractive not just because it was the work of an early Percy: it was at once a marvel to be admired and a mystery to be explored. Why, in this wood edging the River Coquet, had a chapel, a confessional, and a dormitory been hewn out of the solid rock, and the chapel adorned with a groined ceiling as though it were a miniature cathedral? Who was the first inhabitant? Most of all, who were represented in the carved figures in the window niche, particularly those of a woman lying as if in death and of a man standing over her at her feet?

In 1858 Charles H. Hartshorne conjectured that the chapel was built by Henry Percy, second lord of Warkworth, as a chantry where masses could be sung for the soul of his dead wife, Mary, granddaughter of Henry III, and that the two figures represented Henry and Mary.[67] Many have thought them simply a nativity scene.[68] But Percy was not among them, and in the absence of certainty his imagination was stimulated. "It is universally agreed," he writes in the "Advertisement," that the founder of the hermitage "was one of the BERTRAM family," and it has been thought that he was the same Bertram who endowed Brinkburn Priory in the reign of Henry I. But the Gothic windows in the hermitage chapel are in the style of Edward III, and the crest "at the Lady's feet on the tomb" suggests that the sculpture cannot be much older since armorial crests became hereditary only about the time of Edward II. "These appearances," Percy concludes, confirm the account given in his poem and prove that the Hermit of Warkworth was a later member of the Bertram family than the person who founded Brinkburn Priory in the twelfth century (vii). Percy, in fact, sets his scene in the early fifteenth century, with the hermit's reminiscences taking him back some fifty years.

In the poem Bertram tells his story to Henry Percy, eldest son of Hotspur who has been exiled to Scotland by Henry IV, and to Eleanor, half-sister of Henry IV. The two young lovers are hoping that the king and Eleanor's parents will be reconciled with young Percy, but at the start of the poem they have become separated and lost in the woods, where Bertram discovers them. He takes them into the hermitage and, touched by their story, recounts how he, a close friend of Hotspur's father, wooed Isabel Widdrington but was told that he must prove himself in battle

against the Scots before she would accept him. He fought
valiantly with Earl Percy against Douglas, but was wounded;
and when he had recovered and, attended by his brother, went
to seek her, he learned that she had been remorsefully seeking
him for six days. To assist their search, the brother went north,
and Bertram, disguised as a minstrel, went westward through
Scotland until at last a pilgrim informed him of a castle where
the pilgrim thought he had heard a lady's voice "Lamenting
in the tower." Bertram found the castle and was denied admittance. But on the third night of watching he saw a rope ladder
hanging from the wall;

> And soon he saw his love descend
>   Wrapt in a tartan plaid;
> Assisted by a sturdy youth
>   In highland garb y-clad.   (37)

Amazed at the sight, and enraged by Isabel's hanging upon the
youth's arm "With fond familiar air," he pursued them, drew his
sword, "And laid the stranger low."

> Die, traitor, die! – A deadly thrust
>   Attends each furious word.
> Ah! then fair Isabel knew his voice,
>   And rush'd beneath his sword.
>
> O stop, she cried, O stop thy arm!
>   Thou dost thy brother slay!   (38)

   Isabel, Bertram informed his listeners, assured him as she
died that she had remained true to him, and he himself, dis-
suaded by priests from taking his own life, changed his name
from bold Sir Bertram,

> Impetuous, haughty, wild;
> [To] . . . poor and humble BENEDICT,
>   Now lowly, patient, mild.   (43)

He gave his lands "to feed the poor./ And sacred altars raise,"
came to this "sweet sequestered vale" an anchorite, and was

granted the "blest retreat" of the hermitage by Lord Percy: "And here I carv'd her beauteous form,/ and scoop'd this holy cave" (p. 44). As for young Henry and Eleanor, they retired to Scotland on the hermit's advice, and in due time the reconciliation they sought was effected.

This melodramatic narrative of some two hundred ballad stanzas was popular in its day and has had occasional later admirers. Three editions were published in the first year alone; and as late as 1858 Hartshorne could declare that it "will continue to receive admiration as long as there exists a feeling for what is natural and pathetic.... Few ballads ... are recommended by more intrinsic merit."[69] Hartshorne's delight, however, proved less infectious than the wit of Johnson's parody, which will be considered in a later chapter; and certainly it is difficult not to share Johnson's view that stanzas like those of Percy's poem were products of the author's ingenuity rather than creations of a poetic imagination. The poem, in short, can be read with some interest but not with much delight. Its stanzas have none of the dramatic excitement, the cogency of phrase and vividness of imagery, or the music and rhythm of the better English ballads, either from the earlier period or of such Romantic poets as Coleridge and Keats. On the contrary, they are pedestrian almost throughout, with the result that nothing in them seems indispensable or uniquely appropriate.

Percy's connection with the Northumberland family prompted him to write a number of short pieces concerned with the history of the Percys or with Northumberland, as well as to perform a variety of incidental literary services. An article on instances of longevity signed "D. C." (dean of Carlisle) was published in the *Antiquarian Repertory* in 1780 and later supplemented with a note on the longevity of vicars at Worfield near Bridgnorth.[70] The same issue carried "An Account of Percy's Cross" based upon a visit made to that Northumberland monument on August 24, 1765, during Percy's first summer at Alnwick.[71] He probably wrote the account of the duchess of Northumberland published in the newspapers after her death on December 5, 1776, and he clearly prepared her commemorative inscription in the Chapel of St. Nicholas at Westminster Abbey.[72] He corresponded faithfully with Lord Percy, who had been Lord

Warkworth until 1766, when this elder son of the duke of
Northumberland was a general officer in the British forces attempting to suppress the revolution in America, and in 1781 he
was chiefly responsible for drawing up the arguments in support
of Lord Percy's claim to be Great Chamberlain of England.[73]

A more substantial project was his revision of the 194-page
article "Percy. Duke of Northumberland" in the 1768 edition of
Arthur Collins's *The Peerage of England*. The revision, published
in 1779 in volume 2 of the fifth edition (280–490), was a labor
more of duty than of love, although Percy was indefatigable
in writing to fellow antiquarians in quest of records which would
permit him authoritatively to correct some of the numerous
errors in the 1768 account. He was also pleased to be able to
insert new material about his patron, including details of the
duke's improvements to Alnwick Castle, and to write at length
about that branch of the family from which Percy believed himself to have been descended. Nonetheless, he found himself
hemmed in by the account, irritated by the sheer quantity of
its errors, and frustrated by his inability to strike out in his own
way on the history of the Percy family that had attracted him
as early as 1764. On November 7, 1778, he apologized to Treadway Nash for his delay in sending materials on the Percys of
Worcester for Nash's projected *History and Antiquities of Worcestershire*: "I had scarcely made a beginning, when I was
obliged to give up my whole Time to a new Subject recommended
to me by the Duke my Patron, which would admit of no delay."
He had been working night and day, he informed Nash, so that
the publishers of Collins's *Peerage* would not reprint "the old
Blunders," but, persuaded that it will be but a dull business after
all "from the wretched Plan of that dry insipid Work," he had proposed to the duke a sketch of a new history "in a different & more
lively manner." The duke, in fact, was so pleased with the proposal
that Percy had felt compelled to undertake it at the same time
that he was revising the Collins article, and three sheets of the
new work had already been printed. The duke, he added, reads
every proof as it comes from the press and thus leaves him no
alternative to continuing, "lest he sh^d think me careless & inat-
tentive to what gives him Entertainment." As a consequence, he
concluded, "I am at once writing two Books, each of them more
than enough to fill up all my time."[74]

Only nine days away from his appointment as dean of Carlisle when he wrote to Nash on November 7, 1778, Percy never got beyond four sheets of his proposed octavo volume. The thirty-two pages of the four sheets are extant, however, just as the delighted duke of Northumberland must have read them.[75] Entitled *A Genealogical History of the Percy Family,* they trace the family from the Norman chieftains who accompanied William the Conqueror to Maude de Percy, countess of Warwick, who died in 1205. Consistent with Percy's intent, the *Genealogical History* was freed from much of the language of the article. It was by no means freed from all, however, perhaps because of the haste with which Percy was forced to work; it followed the revision of Collins much more closely, in fact, than Percy's comments to Nash would suggest. On the other hand, he did put much of the account in his own words, he changed the order of some sections and expanded a few of them, and he supplied information not to be found in the revision of Collins. If the *Genealogical History* is not the "lively" account that Percy hoped for, it probably came close to what he would have written if, instead of being pressed for time, he had been able to follow his own inclination in preparing his article for the 1779 edition of Collins's *Peerage of England.*

VI *Other Unfinished Works*

Of the numerous works that Percy contracted for between 1761 and 1765, five remained unfinished or unpublished: editions of the *Tatler, Spectator,* and *Guardian,* Buckingham's works, and Surrey's poems as they had been originally published in *Tottel's Miscellany.* All were to have been published by Jacob Tonson, whose death on March 31, 1767, doubtless contributed to Percy's failure to complete them. Tonson had proved a tireless searcher for books to assist Percy in preparing his editions, and he had been the London contact who passed on the old plays which David Garrick lent to Percy for use in compiling a new key to Buckingham's *Rehearsal.* Percy must have felt very keenly the loss of Tonson's encouragement and assistance.

But Tonson's death was not the sole reason for the failure of these efforts. In 1777 Percy relinquished the editorship of the *Tatler, Spectator,* and *Guardian* to John Calder because, as he wrote to John Nichols on May 16, 1783, his work as domestic chaplain and secretary to the duke of Northumberland had left him insufficient leisure for "so voluminous a piece of editorship."[76] With Nichols's assistance, Calder completed all three; the *Tatler* was published in 1786, the *Spectator* (with a number of Percy notes) in 1788, and the *Guardian* in 1789. As for the editions of Buckingham and Surrey, Percy noted in a letter to Horace Walpole dated August 11, 1792, that the sheets of both had been printed earlier, but that since the death of Tonson, "who ought to have assigned them to other persons, they have been wholly discontinued." He added that, with his own fondness for these projects having abated, he had laid them aside until he could offer them to some younger editor, and had now given all the sheets to his own "ingenious nephew," Thomas Percy of St. John's College, Oxford.[77]

Whether or not Percy's interest in the two projects waned, it is doubtful that his nephew ever contributed appreciably to either. More help came from Percy's secretary, H. E. Boyd, who compiled a glossary for the Surrey edition, and George Steevens, who provided specimens of early nondramatic blank verse for a special section of the same edition until he quarreled with Percy in 1797.[78] Percy, in short, continued to collect materials for both editions and hoped to assure their publication at last, and he came so close that in April, 1807, the *Gentleman's Magazine*—edited by John Nichols, who was printing additional material for both editions—announced the imminent publication of Surrey's poems (347). But on February 8, 1808, calamity struck in the form of a fire that destroyed Nichols's warehouse in Red Lion Passage and all its contents, including the sheets representing over forty years' work on the two editions.

Fortunately a few copies of the nearly completed editions survived because they were not in the warehouse at the time of the fire. Percy had also retained the corrected proof sheets, and these are now among the substantial Percy collection in the Bodleian Library. Along with Percy's correspondence related to the *Tatler, Spectator,* and *Guardian* editions, they make it possible to consider the quality of Percy's scholarship in the only other literary efforts of his career which, for sheer ambition and importance, can be said to have rivaled the *Reliques of Ancient English Poetry.*

In each of these Percy sought to supply an authentic text based on a collation of early editions and a consideration of changes known to have been approved by the author. Among your materials, he wrote to John Nichols when the printing of Addison and Steele's volumes devolved upon Nichols in 1783,

you will find one 12mo copy, collated throughout, with the original papers; and you have also the said original papers bound up in volumes, as also complete copies of the octavo editions, which ought generally to be your text, except in such numbers of the Spectator, Tatler, and Guardian as were republished by Tickel in the four volumes of Addison's Works, 4to, where it may be supposed the latest improvements of Addison's pen are correctly given.[79]

Editing Surrey's works required that Percy locate as many editions of *Tottel's Miscellany* as he could, and though, as Cleanth Brooks has suggested, he seems to have mistaken the Bodleian Library's unique copy of the first edition for a later edition of the same year, he had examined six editions by the time of Tonson's death in 1767.[80]

Among Buckingham's works the text most difficult to settle was that of *The Rehearsal,* of which five editions had been published in Buckingham's lifetime. Percy noted in a letter to Thomas Warton dated November 19, 1761, that he had copies of the first, fourth, and fifth editions,[81] but two years were to elapse before he could obtain the missing second and third. On June 28, 1763, Tonson wrote that an advertisement had brought him the second edition,[82] and on October 9 of that year Percy informed Richard Farmer that he had "now got together" copies of all five.[83]

Determining what works to include was not a problem with the *Tatler, Spectator,* and *Guardian* essays, which had been numbered and dated at the time of first publication, but it occupied much of Percy's time with the Surrey and Buckingham editions. On February 20, 1762, Tonson helped confirm a Percy suspicion that Anthony à Wood, in attributing *A Demonstration of the Deity* to Buckingham, had confused it with a Buckingham work entitled *A Short Discourse upon the Reasonableness of Men's Having a Religion, or Worship of God;*[84] and a decision to incorporate "Specimens of Non-Dramatic Blank Verse prior to *Paradise Lost"* into the second volume of Surrey's works protracted the search for materials almost to the moment of the book's destruction.

Annotation was only a minor problem with the *Tatler, Spectator,* and *Guardian,* since Tonson's determination to limit the volumes to the number in the original editions meant that there was little room for notes. These were to be confined largely to identifying concealed authors and briefly illustrating and explaining "forgotten customs and manners, obscure references, and local and temporary or personal allusions."[85] To these ends Percy not only read widely, but he also sought information through correspondence with such persons as John Hoadly, Joseph Warton, Bishop Warburton, and the first and second Lords Hardwicke.[86] With the Surrey edition and much of the Buckingham, annotation was not a problem at all, an agreement having been reached with Tonson to print an unannotated text. With one work, however—Buckingham's *Rehearsal*—annotation was of critical importance, and Percy set out to make a special contribution in that part of his edition.

As a satire on the early Restoration drama, *The Rehearsal* required precise explanation if it was to be fully appreciated by readers no longer familiar with the numerous plays reflected in its satire. A *Key to the Rehearsal* published in 1704 was manifestly inadequate—"erroneous and defective," Percy called it— and he attempted with obvious relish to fill an obvious need.[87] Garrick placed his collection of plays at Percy's disposal, and less than seventeen months after signing his agreement with Tonson, Percy could write to David Dalrymple that he had read all the plays in Garrick's collection between 1660 and 1672, the year that *The Rehearsal* was published.[88] His diary reveals that he read five plays on May 18, 1761, alone; and in one of his manuscripts he listed 177 plays that he had read "with a view to composing the New Key to the Rehearsal."[89] The play and the new key, though never formally to be published, were printed by Tonson no later than the spring of 1765, for on May 9 of that year Thomas Birch, who had supplied a number of materials for a life of Buckingham which Percy originally planned for the edition, thanked him for "the present of your elegant Edition of the *Rehearsal* with the *new Key* to it."[90]

The *New Key to the Rehearsal* was clearly the high point of

the proposed edition; in accuracy, thoroughness, and perception
it exceeded its predecessor at every turn. The earlier *Key,* for
example, had cited lines from two plays of Sir William Killigrew
which Buckingham may have attempted to ridicule in the following from *The Rehearsal's* second act: "Hey day, hey day!/ I
know not what to do, nor what to say!" Percy found lines in
three other plays which Buckingham could also have had in
mind: James Howard's *All Mistaken,* Richard Flecknoe's *Erminia,*
and Sir Aston Cokayne's *Trappolin Supposed a Prince.* Additional
lines and plays cited by Percy but overlooked in the 1704 *Key*
could be multiplied many times, and their effect, had they been
published, would have been to underscore Buckingham's intimate
knowledge of his contemporary theater as well as the continuing
significance of his satire. It is regrettable that, as the delay in
publication lengthened from years into decades, Percy did not
detach the *New Key* and the play from the rest and publish
them separately, but of course it was never possible for him
to foresee how much longer the delay would last.

Percy's instincts in all these editions were sound ones, and
so accurate and perceptive was he that, had he been able to see
the editions through to publication, he could have built a memorable scholarly reputation on them alone. Yet regrettable as it
was that he was kept from completing the editions of Surrey,
Buckingham, and Addison and Steele, the years in which they
were undertaken can hardly be said to have gone to waste.
Taken together, the primary works described in this chapter—
*Hau Kiou Choaan, Miscellaneous Pieces Relating to the Chinese,
The Matrons, Five Pieces of Runic Poetry, The Song of Solomon,
A Key to the New Testament, Northern Antiquities, The Regulation and Establishment of the Houshold of Henry Algernon
Percy,* and *The Hermit of Warkworth*—constituted such an
achievement for a single decade as to assure Percy a place
among the leading scholars of his time. They appear all the more
extraordinary when one considers that they were not Percy's
major preoccupation of the decade, and that, in the midst of this
almost incredible activity, he completed and revised the three
volumes known to subsequent generations as *Percy's Reliques.*

CHAPTER 4

The Reliques of Ancient English Poetry

THE eighteenth-century ballad revival has been so intimately associated with the *Reliques of Ancient English Poetry* that it has been easy to overlook the fact that Percy's compilation marks the end of an era of ballad interest as well as a beginning.[1] Most students of the period are familiar with Joseph Addison's 1711 *Spectator* papers, numbers 70 and 74, which dignified "Chevy Chase" with both high praise and serious critical analysis. Fewer are aware of the published volumes of verse that Percy, assisted by William Shenstone, turned over page by page in search of the gems that would help to distinguish his collection. Without them the *Reliques* would not merely have been different. It might never have come into existence at all.

I *The Background of the* Reliques

Of the 175 poems in the first edition of the *Reliques*, only about fifty can be traced directly to the folio manuscript which was the starting point of Percy's work. For the rest Percy had to seek elsewhere, and even for those in his own manuscript he welcomed the opportunity to collate and compare which the discovery of other versions permitted. Of the poems or alternate versions not yet known to him, some could be found only in manuscripts preserved in such archives as the Bodleian Library, the British Museum, and the library of Magdalene College at Cambridge, where Percy devoted eleven days in August, 1761, to transcribing ballads from the extraordinary Pepys collection of black-letter broadsides.[2] Others might be tucked away in published volumes of the late seventeenth and early eighteenth centuries which brought together songs, ancient ballads, and broadsides, at times in indiscriminate profusion, but always with the possibility that even the crudest mass might yield an occasional diamond. Three of the best-known ballads, "Johnnie Armstrong," "Little Musgrave," and "The Miller and the King's Daughter," had been published in *Wit Restor'd* as early as 1658 and reprinted in *Wit and Drollery* in 1682; and in Henry Bold's *Latine Songs* of 1685 a number of ballads, draped in the rich velvet of classical Latin, peered uncomfortably at their humbler English counterparts on facing pages. One ballad so transformed was "Chevy Chase"— "Ludus Chevinus" in its Latin finery—which, according to Bold, had been raised to its exalted state by order of the bishop of London![3] Thomas D'Urfey's *Pills to Purge Melancholy,* tapped by Percy for some half a dozen ballad texts, saw the old century out and the new century in with its five volumes published between 1698 and 1714, and in 1702 the publisher Jacob Tonson helped the eighteenth century off to a good start with one of his several *Poetical Miscellanies,* where "Chevy Chase" in both native and Roman costumes rubbed shoulders with a number of songs from the seventeenth-century "drolleries" and "garlands." 'Ludus Chevinus," surprisingly enough, was to be reprinted another three times before the end of the decade, and, as Albert Friedman notes, Bold's Latin translation may have inspired Addison to cite a number of classical parallels in his analysis of the English ballad.[4]

The primary object of Percy's quest was what has come to be known as the traditional or popular ballad. This was the type of early English or Scottish poem that Percy, born too soon to be schooled in folk-ballad theory, looked upon as the work of the minstrels, those "genuine successors of the ancient Bards who united the arts of Poetry and Music, and sung verses to the harp, of their own composing."[5] The quest was his major effort in the grandiose project of recovering the ancient poetry of various nations, and that fact accounts in part for his concern to date the ballads in the *Reliques* and to distinguish the minstrel ballads from the printed broadsides of a later date. The single-sheet broadsides had flourished as the art of printing developed and the English reading public increased, but their partisan political bent, their frequent bawdiness and scurrility, and their sheer numbers had brought the ballad into such disrepute in fashionable circles that Percy was never quite ready

to admit that his work was anything but an idle amusement—
"a relaxation from graver studies," as he described it in his 1765
preface (I, xiv).

The word "ballad" was often applied to poems that we would
not consider ballads today, and Percy himself did not always
discriminate. Anything that could be sung or that contained a
narrative might be termed a ballad. In his *Dictionary* Johnson
defined "ballad" as simply "A song" and quoted in illustration
a deprecating comment of Isaac Watts: "*Ballad* once signified
a solemn and sacred song, as well as trivial, when Solomon's
Song was called the *ballad of ballads*; but now it is applied to
nothing but trifling verse." In the cheaply printed seventeenth-
century collections, poems of all kinds tended to be lumped
together as ballads; and in volume 1 of the *Reliques* the book
entitled "Ballads that illustrate Shakespeare" includes lyrics like
"A Song to the Lute in Musicke" and "Take Those Lips Away."
Nor could Percy always readily distinguish between the ballad
of later invention—the broadside—and the minstrel ballad, since
a number of the early ballads were printed in broadsides in the
seventeenth and eighteenth centuries, and the origins of many
were so obscure as to be quite indeterminate. Of "Chevy Chase"
Percy published both a "minstrel" version printed by Thomas
Hearne in 1719 from an Ashmole Library manuscript and the
later broadside version praised by Addison in his *Spectator* papers
(I, 1–17; 231–46).

In consultation with William Shenstone, Percy systematically
leafed through such collections as Allan Ramsay's *Tea-Table
Miscellany* (1723) and *The Evergreen* (1724), Elizabeth
Cooper's *The Muses Library* (1737), Edward Capell's *Prolusions*
(1760), and the anonymously compiled *The Hive* (1721) and
The Vocal Miscellany (1734).[6] The anonymous *Collection of
Old Ballads* (1723–1725) contained the texts of some twenty-
five poems later published in the *Reliques*, although many of
them had come to Percy's attention through other compilations
as well. The format of the *Collection*—three volumes, with each
containing early and late poems arranged in chronological order
—was essentially the format that Percy adopted for the *Reliques*,
although he gave it considerably more variety and interest by
dividing each volume into three sections with separate chrono-

logical developments, and by grouping a number of poems with common themes or origins: Northumberland ballads, for example, mad songs, and ballads that illustrate Shakespeare. In the quality of its selections, the *Collection of Old Ballads,* which concentrated upon historical ballads, was in no way a match for the *Reliques.*[7]

Ballads, then, even if they lacked the stature of other kinds of poetry, were a commonplace of eighteenth-century English life long before Percy became aware of them; and, only a few years before the *Reliques,* James Macpherson's publication of the so-called Erse fragments had raised the interest in the poetry of ancient Britain to a new pitch. If Macpherson helped to direct Percy's attention to Scotland, from which he drew more than a dozen ballads for the *Reliques,* Percy's own alertness and curiosity, as well as a singular stroke of good luck, can be credited with arousing his interest in balladry in the first place. In a note which he inscribed on the flyleaf of his folio manuscript on November 7, 1769, Percy explained how the manuscript had come into his possession some years earlier:

This very curious old Manuscript in its present mutilated state, but unbound and sadly torn &c., I rescued from destruction, and begged at the hands of my worthy friend Humphrey Pitt Esq., then living at Shiffnal in Shropshire, afterwards of Priorslee, near that town; who died very lately at Bath (viz. in Summer 1769). I saw it lying dirty on the floor under a Bureau in ye Parlour: being used by the Maids to light the fires.[8]

Pitt was the uncle of the Reverend Robert Binnel, who had assisted Percy with the *Song of Solomon* and joined with him in contributing to Grainger's edition of Tibullus. Probably Percy came upon the manuscript sometime during his curacies of Astley abbots and Tasley, when he would have been in frequent company with his Shropshire friends; that is, between late 1751 and early 1756. Although he had had presence enough to shield the manuscript from the searing hands of Humphrey Pitt's maids, Percy confessed that he did not at first recognize its full value. As a result he had himself torn out one or two of its pages and sent the manuscript to a binder, who trimmed the top and bottom margins so closely that some parts of the text were cut

away.[9] As for publication, it was Johnson who first impressed
Percy with the manuscript's possibilities. In the opening letter
of his correspondence with Shenstone, written on November 24,
1757, Percy noted that he had the manuscript in his possession
and that Johnson had expressed a desire to see it printed.[10] On
December 20 of that year he compiled a list of the manuscript's
contents, and he began the actual work of editing the following
summer.[11]

Once owned by Thomas Blount, author of the 1679 *Jocular
Tenures*, the folio manuscript seems to have been compiled about
1650 by a Lancashire native of diverse tastes.[12] Its 500 pages
included seventeen romances, twenty-four metrical histories,
about a hundred miscellaneous songs, some broadside ballads,
and forty-five which the great nineteenth-century ballad scholar
Francis Child classified as popular ballads. Of these a number
are incomplete: "The Marriage of Sir Gawaine," for example,
had six gaps of nine stanzas each. Printing such a manuscript,
or selections from it, might have afforded Percy a welcome challenge; an attempt to fill in the gaps, fruitless though it might
at times have proved, would alone have required the kind of
search in manuscript and printed sources that he delighted in.
But in conference with Shenstone, Percy steadily worked out
a plan to supplement selected ballads and songs from his own
manuscript with others of similar merit, and to edit them in such
a way as to make them acceptable to the general reading public.
The book, originally projected in two volumes but later extended
to three, was thus seen as an anthology of English poetry, with
emphasis upon the early ballads of the minstrels and the lyrics
of such sixteenth- and seventeenth-century poets as Shakespeare,
Marlowe, Jonson, Suckling, Carew, and Crashaw. *Reliques of
Ancient English Poetry: Consisting of Old Heroic Ballads, Songs,
and Other Pieces of Our Earlier Poets, (Chiefly of the Lyric Kind.)
Together with Some Few of Later Date*—such was its complete
title. Because of their length, the romances of Percy's manuscript
were to be excluded, as were the longest of the ballads and those
which offended morality and decency. The restriction to English
poetry was not so rigorously enforced as to exclude Scottish
ballads or even Percy's own translations of the Spanish "Rio
Verde, Rio Verde" and "Alcanzor and Zayda," the first of which
was printed with its Spanish original.

Percy was in touch with Shenstone at just about every step of the way. Indeed, as more than one writer has noted, Percy always seemed happy to find someone to help him make decisions; and his reliance on Shenstone was so extensive that he tended to think of his friend as a partner rather than a consultant in his enterprise. He took very seriously the ratings which Shenstone assigned to each of the poems in the collections they perused, even though he did not always concur in them. From Shenstone came advice on the importance of alternating long and short poems, on organization, on the illustrations and the layout, and even on the desirability of an uncrowded title page.[13] Shenstone's continuing concern, however, was that the antiquarian in Percy not select poems only for their antiquity, and that the scholar not edit the collection in such a way as to discourage readers of taste.[14] Referring to the way in which corrupt and fragmentary texts might be handled, he wrote to Percy on October 1, 1760, as follows:

I believe I shall *never* make any objection to such *Improvements* as you bestow upon them; unless you were plainly to *contradict* Antiquity, which I am pretty sure will never be the Case.

As to alterations of a *word or two*, I do not esteem it a point of *Conscience* to *particularize them* on *this* occasion. Perhaps, where a whole *Line* or *More* is alter'd, it may be proper enough to give some Intimation of it. The Italick type may answer this purpose, if you do not employ it on other occasions. It will have the appearance of a modern *Toe* or *Finger*, which is *allowably* added to the best old Statues: And I think I should always let the Publick imagine, that these were owing to *Gaps*, rather than to *faulty Passages*. (72–73)

Percy, whose initial preference was for a minimally corrected text, was to go beyond the limits contemplated by Shenstone in this letter, with consequences which will be considered later in this chapter.

II *Publishing the* Reliques

With his preliminary work behind him, the indefatigable Percy set out in 1761 to secure the keys that would open the country's remaining ballad sources to him. On April 13, 1761, more than a month before signing a contract with Robert Dodsley—"Sold

Dodsley my old Ballads," Percy recorded in his diary on May 22—he applied for admission to the Reading Room of the British Museum, where he was to find a dozen ballad texts he later made use of in the *Reliques*.[15] On May 28 he sent off a letter informing Thomas Warton at Oxford of his project and inquiring about materials in the Oxford libraries and the possibility of obtaining access to them. On July 21 he began a long correspondence with the Welsh scholar Evan Evans, and by May of 1762 he was exchanging friendly letters with Richard Farmer at Cambridge. On November 10, 1762, he introduced himself by letter to David Dalrymple in Edinburgh, Shenstone's efforts to gain the assistance of John McGowan having been largely unavailing, at least for the time being.[16] Evans understandably lent his best assistance with works like *Five Pieces of Runic Poetry* and *Northern Antiquities* rather than with the *Reliques*, but Warton and Farmer proved to be indispensable contacts at the two universities, and Dalrymple, in addition to other help, supplied such treasures from Scottish balladry that Percy dislodged a number of poems from his original contents in order to accommodate them.[17] At Cambridge Percy was also aided by Edward Blakeway of Magdalene College, where his eleven days in the Pepysian Library yielded some three dozen texts for his collection.

The death of Shenstone on February 11, 1763, was a heavy blow to Percy, and one of his first impulses was to dedicate the *Reliques* to Shenstone's memory.[18] But on March 10, 1764, as the work neared completion, he wrote to Elizabeth Percy, countess of Northumberland, to ask if she would accept the dedication.[19] The change was an understandable one. Whether or not the idea was Percy's own, one can imagine that he would have needed little encouragement to approach this colorful and influential Percy matriarch. She was a natural choice: descendant of ancient Percys renowned in history, song, and ballad, and, Percy noted, "In her own right Baroness Percy, Lucy, Poynings, Fitz-Payne, Bryan, and Latimer." For Percy her acceptance of the dedication proved to be one of the happier strokes of fortune in a life generally subject to good fortune. It helped to assure his book, this parcel of old ballads that he never ceased to feel uneasy about, a ready passage into fashionable circles, and it marked the beginning of a long and intimate connection with the

Northumberland family which brought an almost undreamed of fulfillment of Percy's literary, clerical, social, and financial aspirations. Percy was to retain his two Northamptonshire churches until he became bishop of Dromore in 1782, but in 1765 the modest vicarage at Easton Mauduit began the process of surrendering its occupant to Northumberland House and Alnwick Castle.

With the Northumberland stamp on his efforts assured, Percy felt impelled to revise his three volumes in order to give greater prominence to the Northumberland poems. Already in type, these were the major element of his third volume, and to accomplish his purpose he simply interchanged volumes 1 and 3. Thus the entire set of three volumes was aptly led off by "The Ancient Ballad of Chevy-Chase" and "The Battle of Otterbourne," with "An Elegy on Henry 4th Earl of Northumberland" closing the first book of volume 1, and "The More Modern Ballad of Chevy-Chase," "The Rising in the North," and "Northumberland Betrayed by Douglas" dominating the third. Among the longest and most notable poems in the collection, they record the deeds and misdeeds of the house of Percy and trumpet the relentless and at times impetuous valor of Harry Hotspur and his Northumberland followers.

Percy spent most of June, 1764, on the details of interchanging the first and third volumes, and on June 25 Samuel Johnson arrived at Easton Mauduit with Mrs. Anna Williams on a long-promised visit.[20] During Johnson's seven-week stay, Percy sought his assistance in explicating some of the more obscure words in the glossaries—one for each volume of the *Reliques*—which he finally had to send off to David Dalrymple in Edinburgh with a plea for help.[21] But Johnson's major assistance was in writing the dedication to the countess of Northumberland, a role which was not to be disclosed until 1791, when Boswell, having canceled at Percy's request a page of his *Life of Johnson* attributing the dedication to Johnson, neglected to delete the index reference to it.[22] The dedication, Percy later acknowledged, "owed its finest strokes" to Johnson's pen.[23] It may, in fact, be said to consist largely of fine strokes in the Johnson manner, and it has long been given a place in the canon of Johnson's works.[24]

On November 22, 1764, Percy waited on the countess of

Northumberland and presented her with an advance copy of the three-volume set.[25] On February 11, 1765, copies were made available to the public at a cost, bound, of half a guinea.[26] Although the book was treated somewhat condescendingly in the April *Gentleman's Magazine,* it was reviewed favorably and at length in the February *Critical Review* and the April *Monthly Review.*[27] But perhaps the best measure of the *Reliques's* initial success is that James Dodsley, the sole proprietor of the publishing firm since his brother's death in 1764, contracted to pay Percy two hundred guineas, probably for a second edition, only a little more than a month after the book's publication.[28] "The Reliques sell far better than I could have expected," Percy wrote to David Dalrymple a week later on March 23, 1765. "Dodsley has already had 600 sets fetched away." And on July 2 Percy informed Thomas Warton that 1,100 copies of the total impression of 1,500 had been sold.[29]

III   *The Success of the* Reliques

The countess of Northumberland may have helped to introduce the *Reliques* into circles which might otherwise have neglected it, but it was out of her power to assure its success. For that, Percy had to depend largely on his own abilities, although his task was eased to no small extent by the changing tastes of the times. In its Gothic focus the *Reliques* bore a clear relationship to Macpherson's Ossian poems (1760), Hurd's *Letters on Chivalry and Romance* (1762), Walpole's *Castle of Otranto* (1764) and his mansion at Strawberry Hill, poems like Gray's "The Bard" (1757), and even Percy's modest runic translations; and, if such works as these had not already stimulated a general enthusiasm, they pointed clearly to that consuming public interest in the Gothic which was to characterize the following century.

The *Reliques* was itself disarmingly modest, at least in appearance. Its three volumes pressed lightly on the hand, and, attractively printed and illustrated as they were, they came close to being models of the bookmaker's art. To many of Percy's contemporaries, however, they must at first glance have seemed a mere collection of poems such as they were accustomed to finding occasionally in their bookstalls, with the obvious dif-

ference that these were mostly old and in language eccentric
and at times obscure—"Ancient Songs and Ballads," as the running heads proclaimed across each double page. But if they read
the poems, as of course many did, they discovered very quickly
that the language was not quite so perplexing as it seemed, that
it had in fact a charm of its own, and that it was conveying
stories and songs of extraordinary variety and interest. For
Percy, together with Shenstone, had taken infinite pains in the
selection and placement of individual poems, with a view to
holding the reader's attention both on the poem itself and on the
collection as a whole.

It helped, of course, that the three volumes did not look
forbiddingly crowded: individual poems and lines of verse were
well spaced; the footnotes, mostly textual, were neither numerous
nor long; the page margins were substantial. But, what was
more important, the poems were both related to each other and
constantly varied. The two long ballads which open the first
book of volume 1, for example—"The Ancient Ballad of Chevy-
Chase," thirteen pages in length exclusive of Percy's commentary,
and "The Battle of Otterbourne," ten and a half pages—are followed by "The Jew's Daughter" (2 pages), which, though allied
with them in violence through its story of the Christian child
murdered by the Jews, affords as striking a contrast with its
predecessors in spirit as it does in length. The first book is then
filled out with "Sir Cauline" (17 pages), "Edward, Edward"
(2½ pages), "King Estmere" (12 pages), "Sir Patrick Spence"
(2 pages), "Robin Hood and Guy of Gisborne" (10 pages), "The
Tower of Doctrine" (3 pages), "The Child of Elle" (8½ pages),
and "Edom o'Gordon" (6½ pages). In addition to its changing
lengths and themes, the first book was given added variety by its
lyric poems—Stephen Hawes' "The Tower of Doctrine" and John
Skelton's "Elegy on Henry 4th Earl of Northumberland," which
followed "Edom o'Gordon"—and by four ballads clearly designated as Scottish and interspersed among the six English ballads
and the two lyrics.

The first book, moreover, in which the Northumberland Percys
were dominant characters and valor and courage were recurring
but not exclusive themes, was followed by a second book devoted
to ballads that illustrate Shakespeare. Arranged in chronological

order like those in the first book, the sixteen poems of book 2 begin with "Adam Bell, Clym of the Clough, and William of Cloudesly," at thirty-one pages the longest by far in the entire collection. They continue through familiar short lyrics like "Willow, Willow, Willow" and "The Passionate Shepherd to His Love" and less familiar ballads like "King Cophetua and the Beggar-Maid" and "The Frolicksome Duke, or the Tinker's Good Fortune," and they conclude with Percy's own "The Friar of Orders Gray," a ballad fashioned out of some of the numerous snatches dispersed through Shakespeare's plays.

The third book resumes the Northumberland ballads, and, having opened it with "The More Modern Ballad of Chevy-Chase" of Elizabethan origin, Percy was constrained by his chronological pattern to confine the book to poems on the whole more recent than those of other books. "Chevy-Chase" is followed by James Shirley's "Death's Final Conquest," the Northumberland poems "The Rising in the North" and "Northumberland Betrayed by Douglas," the anonymous "My Mind to Me a Kingdom Is," and the Elizabethan William Warner's "The Patient Countess." A series of early seventeenth-century poems by such writers as Henry Wotton, Michael Drayton, Samuel Daniel, and Thomas Carew then concludes with the Scottish ballad "Gilderoy," probably dating from the mid-seventeenth century, and from there Percy leaps ahead to the 1726 "Winifreda" and thence to his own time and his own circle. Shenstone is represented by "Jemmy Dawson," "the ingenious Dr. *Harrington*, of Bath" by the 1756 "Witch of Wokey," and James Grainger by a West Indian ballad. Reserving the last word for himself, Percy closes the volume with his own translations from the Spanish, "Gentle River, Gentle River" and "Alcanzor and Zayda, a Moorish Tale."

The second volume consists largely of poems on historical and political subjects, among them "For the Victory at Agincourt," "On Thomas Lord Cromwell," "Queen Elizabeth's Verses, While Prisoner at Woodstock," and "The Murder of the King of Scots." The third, as Percy stated and many of the titles attest, is "chiefly devoted to romantic subjects": "The Boy and the Mantle," "The Knight, and Shepherd's Daughter," "Sweet William's Ghost," "The Children in the Wood," "The Dragon of Wantley." One of its sequences contains poems about "little foot-pages" and other young people; another focuses upon witches, hobgoblins, and fairies. Both the second and the third volumes follow the pattern of the first, with each of their three books developed chronologically, with constant variety in the themes and lengths of poems, and with lyrics spaced among the ballads and Scottish poems among the English. The third book of volume 2 contains a series of six "Mad Songs," madness being a subject, Percy observed, treated more frequently by the English than by their neighbors, although he declined to speculate whether the English were "more liable to this calamity than other nations" (II, 343).

The puffs given to himself and his friends through the insertion in the first volume of one poem each by Shenstone, Grainger, and himself and of two of his own translations were not repeated in subsequent volumes, although Percy's version of "Valentine and Ursine" was included in the third book of volume 3. Under Percy's initial plan, of course, the poems would have closed, not the first volume but the third, where they would have served as a kind of appendix, a relaxed self-indulgence, perhaps, as Percy rested after the labors of his three volumes. They can hardly be said to raise the poetic level of the *Reliques,* but they do help to give it some of its pleasant personal quality. Percy is like the director who cannot resist taking a part in his own production. But contemporary readers must have felt his presence constantly: he was at hand throughout to help them understand and enjoy what they were reading. Most poems have their own, usually brief, introductions and some have postscripts. And four widely separated essays help to unify parts of the collection and to illuminate them historically and critically: "An Essay on the Ancient English Minstrels," "On the Origin of the English Stage," "On the [Alliterative] Metre of Pierce Plowman's Visions," and "On the Ancient Metrical Romances." Together these constitute a brief and selective history of early English poetry, but one much advanced for its time, and it is not surprising that James Dodsley gathered them into a single volume in 1767 and sold them apart from the *Reliques.*[30]

The "Essay on the Ancient English Minstrels" is the key essay as well as the first, for it sets the framework and the tone for much of what follows in the three volumes. The minstrels, as Percy perceives them, are romantic figures: poets, musicians,

members of "a distinct order of men ... [who] got their livelihood by singing verses to the harp, at the houses of the great."
Their verses, of course, were not necessarily their own: "From
the amazing variations, which occur in different copies of these
old pieces, it is evident they made no scruple to alter each other's
productions, and the reciter added or omitted whole stanzas,
according to his own fancy or convenience" (I, xvi). In Anglo-
Saxon times, Percy notes, the minstrel's admission to royal circles
was accepted as a matter of course, and even as late as the reign
of Henry VIII "the Reciters of verses, or moral speeches learnt
by heart, intruded without ceremony into all companies; not only
in taverns, but in the houses of the nobility themselves" (I, xix).
By the end of Queen Elizabeth's reign, however, such men were
included by statute among "rogues, vagabonds, and sturdy beggars" (I, xxi).

As long as the minstrels subsisted, Percy observed, "they seem
never to have designed their rhymes for publication, and probably never committed them to writing themselves: what copies
are preserved ... were doubtless taken down from their mouths."
Their ballads are "in the northern dialect, abound with antique
words and phrases, are extremely incorrect, and run into the
utmost licence of metre; they have also a romantic wildness, and
are in the true spirit of chivalry" (I, xxii).

"I have no doubt," wrote Percy, "but most of the old heroic
ballads in this collection were produced by this order of men"
(I, xvi). The latest such poems he could discover were "The
Rising in the North" and "Northumberland Betrayed by Douglas,"
both of the late sixteenth century. The "genuine old Minstrelsy,"
by then almost extinct, had gradually been replaced by "a new
race of ballad-writers ..., an inferior sort of minor poets, who
wrote narrative songs meerly for the press." Their works, written
in the southern dialect, are "in exacter measure, have a low or
subordinate correctness, sometimes bordering on the insipid ...,
exhibit a more modern phraseology, and are commonly descriptive of more modern manners" (I, xxii–xxiii). Percy's preference
for the older ballads was never in doubt.

"On the Origin of the English Stage" is the introductory essay
for the "Ballads that Illustrate Shakespeare" in the second book
of volume 1. In the essay Percy traces dramatic poetry from the

solemn religious festivals of the Middle Ages through the mystery and morality plays and their sequels. Moralities like *Everyman,* he states, gave birth to modern tragedy, and moralities like *Hick-Scorner* to modern comedy. But "Moralities still kept their ground" and at length became the popular masques of the courts of James I and Charles I. Mysteries ceased to be acted after the Reformation, but seem to have given rise to historical plays, which the "old writers" considered distinct from tragedies and comedies (I, 118–28).

In the essay "On the Metre of Pierce Plowman's Visions," which introduces the third book of volume 2, Percy describes the unrhymed alliterative verse of the Icelandic poets, gives the rules of Icelandic prosody as analyzed by Wormius in his *Literatura Runica* of 1636, and notes that *Pierce Plowman's Visions,* written, he says, by Robert Langland and published shortly after 1350, is "constructed exactly" by those rules.[31] Langland, he observes, was neither the first nor the last English poet to use the alliterative verse; but after rhyme was superadded, it came at last to engross "the whole attention of the poet," with the result that "the internal imbellishment of alliteration was no longer studied," and the rules that Langland wrote by were forgotten. The cadences of alliterative verse, though not the alliteration, says Percy, may still be seen in French heroic verse (II, 260–70).

Percy's final volume opens with the last of his four essays, "On the Ancient Metrical Romances," a subject particularly close to his heart. The romances, he asserts, may be traced back to the historical songs of the ancient Gothic scalds, who celebrated the chivalric ideas long before the Crusades or the adoption of chivalry as a military order. The earliest French romances of chivalry were metrical and date from the eleventh century, whereas the earliest English romance Percy had discovered, "Hornechild," dates from the twelfth. By the fourteenth century metrical romances had become so popular in England that Chaucer burlesqued them in his tale of "Sir Thopas," where he cited a number of romances still extant in manuscript in the eighteenth century. Many of these, Percy observes, illuminate the manners and opinions of their times and have substantial poetic merit; although they cannot be set in competition with Chaucer's works, "they are far more spirited and entertaining than the tedious allegories of Gower, or the dull and prolix legends of Lydgate." He concludes his account by summarizing the nine parts of "Libius Disconius," which he declares as "regular in its conduct, as any of the finest poems of classical antiquity" and worthy of being regarded as an epic (III, ii–xvi). He then appended to the essay a list of thirty metrical romances still extant, with the locations of manuscript and printed texts (III, xvii–xxiv).

In 1876, when Henry B. Wheatley published what continues to be the standard edition of the *Reliques*, he announced in the "Editor's Preface" that to treat the four essays as he had treated Percy's prefaces to individual poems—that is, by merely adding footnotes and terminal comments—"would necessitate so many notes and corrections as to cause confusion; and as the Essays on the English Stage, and the Metrical Romances, are necessarily out of date, the trouble expended would not have been repaid by the utility of the result." He had, accordingly, "thrown them to the end of their respective volumes, where they can be read exactly as Percy left them" (I, xi). In Percy's own day, however, almost no one was aware that the essays were in want of corrective or supplementary notes and comment, or that for such a want they would in time be "thrown" to the rear of their volumes, as accumulations of bric-a-brac are sometimes stuffed into inconspicuous closets. Percy—the first of his countrymen "to inspect actual English medieval romances" or "to demonstrate that alliteration was the principle of Anglo-Saxon and Germanic verse generally"[32]—had carried his readers about as far as was possible for any one person in 1765, and they had reason to be grateful for the sure hand with which he pointed out places of interest along the way. Like his essays, his introductions to the poems were written with whatever authority pioneer research would admit and, in spite of his disclaimer about a parcel of old ballads, with an infectious conviction that the poems in his collection were not simply curios but would repay serious attention with unusual delight. "This excellent old ballad," he says of "The Wandering Prince of Troy,"

. . . is given from the editor's folio MS. collated with two different printed copies, both in black letter in the Pepys collection.

The reader will smile to observe with what natural and affecting simplicity, our ancient ballad-maker has engrafted a Gothic conclusion on the classic story of Virgil, from whom, however, it is probable he had it not. Nor can it be denied, but he has dealt out his poetical justice with a more impartial hand, than that celebrated poet. (III, 192)

In discussing the ballads in the same breath with Chaucer, Spenser, Shakespeare, and, as in this passage, Virgil, Percy was according them a dignity they were seldom given; and in placing them side by side with poems of Ben Jonson, Richard Lovelace, Sir John Suckling, John Dryden, and others, he was providing his readers an opportunity to see that the older poems did not inevitably suffer by comparison and that the roots of the English literary genius struck as deep as English history. The *Reliques* was a work of national pride, and it is not surprising that a nation as proud as Britain took it to its heart.

Wheatley's relegation of the essays to the back pages tends to obscure an important aspect of the *Reliques*. The collection, to be sure, lacked the kind of tight organization which rendered all tampering with it dangerous. Percy spent countless hours putting together the pieces for the first edition, only to move a number of them for the second. More significantly, he found it expedient at the last moment to interchange the first and third volumes, and he accomplished this major structural change with minimum inconvenience and damage. The collection was, of course, an anthology, and like other anthologies it could be dipped into at practically any point. Inevitably that has been one of its attractions. But the *Reliques* also provides incentives for reading it through from beginning to end, and that is in fact the way in which it can be read most profitably. Unquestionably the "Essay on the Ancient English Minstrels" belonged at the head of the book, for it is a kind of Percy manifesto and its spirit pervades the entire work. The sections of each book are units, moreover, short enough and expertly enough selected and varied to be read without tedium in one sitting. They move ahead chronologically, have themes in common, and gain added coherence through the short introductions to separate poems. Even before starting a poem the reader may be invited to read on in the next: "This little moral sonnet," Percy says of James Shirley's "Victorious Men of Earth," "hath such a pointed application to the heroes of the foregoing and following ballads, that I cannot help placing it here, tho' the date of its composition is of a much later period" (II, 222). The generally brief and unpedantic concern for dates, sources, backgrounds, and relationships gives the poems a special luster; Percy fusses over them just enough to make them seem wanted and important. They were largely dredged out of old books and manuscripts, for Percy preceded the era of the ballad hunter who recorded the words and music of rustic men and women singing at the plough or the spinning wheel. But his poems almost never come with the musty odor of old trunks or dank closets. Percy, moreover, although he knew little of music, was not oblivious to the possibilities of oral tradition, even if he did not pursue them assiduously. One is made aware from time to time that some of the best of the poems have been homely favorites of English and Scottish people; of "Gil Morrice," Percy tells us, two Scottish editions were printed from a copy collected "from the mouths of old women and nurses," and he himself is now inserting sixteen additional lines submitted in response to the Scottish editors' request for readers to help improve the text (III, 93).

Percy intrudes without being intrusive; he is informal, even chatty at times, a friend taking a friend into his confidence. He calls attention to another version of "Lord Thomas and Fair Ellinor" in the Pepys collection, an attempt at modernization by reducing the poem to a different measure: "A proof of it's popularity," he assures us (III, 82). He apologizes disarmingly for not placing "The Heir of Linne" earlier in volume 2: it was "owing to an oversight" (II, 309). Many of his introductions provide just enough information to whet his readers' appetites; he expects the poems to satisfy them. And taken all in all, there are not many among the songs and ballads of the *Reliques* that one would wish to replace. If Percy overlooked some of the best of the ballads, he also included many of the best: "Chevy-Chase," "The Battle of Otterbourne," "The Boy and the Mantle," "Sir Patrick Spence," "Edward, Edward," "Child Waters," "Barbara Allen's Cruelty," "The Children in the Wood," "The

Bonny Earl of Murray"—the list is a long one, and it covers a broad range of human experience. No doubt it was this ability of Percy to recapture and not just to disinter the past that prompted Johnson's well known tribute to him: "Percy's attention to poetry has given grace and splendour to his studies of antiquity. A mere antiquarian is a rugged being."[33]

The difference for the *Reliques,* of course, was crucial, and Percy, who was well aware of it, articulated it with some feeling in one of the book's four essays. "It has happened unluckily," he wrote of the old metrical romances,

that the antiquaries, who have revived the works of our ancient writers, have been for the most part men void of taste and genius, and therefore have always fastidiously rejected the old poetical Romances, because founded on fictitious or popular subjects, while they have been careful to grub up every petty fragment of the most dull and insipid rhimist, whose merit it was to deform morality, or obscure true history. (III, ix)

If compiling the *Reliques* did not require the genius of a Johnson, it did require taste and judgment, including an ability on the editor's part to put himself constantly in the reader's position, and these were precisely the qualities that Percy, with Shenstone's encouragement and assistance, was able to bring to his task.

IV   *The Second and Third Editions*

Percy's success with the first edition of the *Reliques* established him as England's leading ballad authority, and it did not take him long to follow up his success with a second edition. It was published by James Dodsley in 1767.[34] With so many excellent poems excluded from the first edition, and with his new-won fame bringing him ballad transcriptions and information from correspondents all over Britain, there must have been considerable temptation for Percy to revise the second edition extensively. He did not, however, perhaps because he hesitated to risk a proven success, and perhaps because he was reserving the best of his unused poems for other projects. Almost to the end of his life, for example, he nursed the idea of a fourth volume of the *Reliques,* a project he contemplated turning over to his son and then, following his son's death, to his nephew. At various times he drew up plans for special collections such as ballads on English history, English romances, and ancient English and Scottish poems.[35]

The changes in the second edition, in any event, seem minimal. Not a single poem in the first edition was deleted from the second, and only three were added. "Jephthah Judge of Israel," called to Percy's attention by George Steevens, was inserted among the "Ballads that Illustrate Shakespeare," where it remained through the third and fourth editions (2d ed., I, 176–79). The second addition was "Jealousy Tyrant of the Mind," identified in the second edition (and the third) as coming from "a Manuscript copy communicated to the Editor," and in the fourth edition as a song by Dryden from *Love Triumphant* (4th ed., III, 273). The third was a French translation of John Lyly's "Cupid and Campaspe" entitled "L'Amour et Glycere," which was written expressly for the *Reliques* by an unnamed friend and placed by Percy at the very end of volume 3. It seems strange that in revising his collection of "Ancient English" poetry Percy should have chosen to conclude it with a poem in modern French, but presumably friendship and the connection with "Cupid and Campaspe," printed earlier in volume 3, overcame any Percy doubts on that point, at least for the second and third editions. Percy omitted the poem in the fourth edition.

A total of eighteen poems were given new positions, although four of these were accounted for by two instances in which poems already adjacent to each other simply exchanged places. One change set up a circular chain reaction. When Percy discovered the printed text of "The Shepherd's Resolution" and thereby learned that George Wither was the author, he substituted the printed text for his fragmentary folio manuscript text and moved the poem from book 2 of volume 3 to the place occupied by "Dulcina" in book 3. "Dulcina" was moved forward seven positions to displace "The Auld Good Man," which in turn was moved forward to the place which had been occupied by "The Shepherd's Resolution." Percy must have gone through many such sequences when he was deciding upon the order of the poems for the first edition.

The other significant changes in the poems also resulted from Percy's use of texts previously unknown to him. The text of "My Mind to Me a Kingdom Is" was revised and the poem's last four stanzas were detached from the first seven and printed separately under the title "The Golden Mean," changes Percy based upon a 1588 publication of William Byrd's psalms, sonnets, and songs. "The Golden Mean" held its place in the third edition but was dropped from the fourth.[36] Punning commendatory verses attributed to King James I were replaced in the second edition by two sonnets of King James because someone had suggested to Percy that "the king only gave the quibbling commendations in prose, and that some obsequious court-rhymer put them into metre" (II, 303–4). Finally, "The Aspiring Shepherd," printed from the folio manuscript, was discovered to be George Wither's "The Stedfast Shepherd," and the entire seven stanzas, correctly titled, were printed in the second edition (III, 263–66) from *The Mistress of Philarete,* which was also Percy's source for the full text of "The Shepherd's Resolution."

Changes in the selections were even less numerous in the third edition, which was published in 1775. Two adjacent poems in the third volume, "Lucy and Colin" and "Margaret's Ghost," were transposed. In the same volume "The Wanton Wife of Bath," which, as Percy noted, Addison in the *Spectator* [No. 247] had pronounced an excellent ballad, was replaced by "The Bride's Burial." No doubt, in spite of Addison's assurance, the Wife of Bath, who at heaven's gate successively asserts her moral superiority to Adam, Jacob, Lot, Judith, David, Solomon, Jonas, Thomas, Mary Magdalen, Paul, and Peter, was a little *too* wanton for Percy's sustained comfort. The saintly virgin bride of "The Bride's Burial" could have posed no problems.

In the third edition Percy notes also that the texts of "Phillida and Corydon" and "The Shepherd's Address to His Muse," printed in volume 3 from a small Elizabethan quarto manuscript in his possession, have been improved by reference to printed copies in *England's Helicon.* The most significant change of this kind, however, occurred in "The Battle of Otterbourne," for which Percy substituted a text from a Cotton Library manuscript called to his attention by the Chaucer scholar Thomas Tyrwhitt.[37] The new text contained fifty-eight lines not found in the Harleian manuscript used by Percy in his first two editions.

In both the second and third editions, Percy occasionally added, deleted, or revised a note, and his changes in the introductions and postscripts to the poems were at times substantial, particularly when the discovery of a new text gave him a new view of the poem or its author. Among his more notable changes in the second edition are those in the annotations to the two "Chevy-Chase" ballads and "The Battle of Otterbourne," where his newly acquired intimacy with Northumberland and the Northumberland family is clearly reflected. He is no longer content, for example, to refer his readers to Fuller's *Worthies* and Crawfurd's *Peerage* (his first edition authorities) for information about the Scottish and Northumberland leaders slain in the bloody battle between Douglas and Hotspur:

> Thear was slayne with the lord Persè
>   Sir John of Agerstone,
> Sir Roger the hinde Hartly,
>   Sir Wyllyam the bold Hearone.
>
> Sir Jorg the worthè Lovele
>   A knyght of great renowen,
> Sir Raff the ryche Rugbè
>   With dyntes wear beaten dowene.
>
>   (2d ed., I, 14)

Instead he provides, at the end of the second poem, a series of comments on each of the persons, or their families, whose names compose the rolls of honor in "The Ancient Ballad of Chevy-Chase" and "The Battle of Otterbourne": Lovele, for example, "*seems to be the ancient family of* Delaval, *of* Seaton Delaval, *in Northumberland,*" and "*The family of* Haggerston *of* Haggerston, *near Berwick, has been seated there for many centuries, and still remains*" (2d ed., I, 32). A similar list follows "The More Modern Ballad of Chevy-Chase" (I, 266–68).[38]

Among the family treasures that the earl and countess of Northumberland brought out for Percy during the first months of their acquaintance was the manuscript of the *Northumberland Houshold Book*, which, as we have seen, Percy was to edit for a private printing in 1770. He began making use of the manuscript, however, in the second edition of the *Reliques*. A half-page extract from it is appended to "Gentle Herdsman, Tell to Me" to show the constant tribute paid to "Our Lady of Walsingham" (II, 399–400). Another, illustrating "the fondness of our ancestors" for miracle plays, constitutes about half of a five-page addition to the essay "On the Origin of the English Stage" (I, 367–69). Percy also finds support in the manuscript for his statement in the "Essay on the Ancient English Minstrels" that "Minstrels were retained in all great and noble families," and in a footnote to the text he observes with obvious pride that the house of Northumberland, which ages ago had three minstrels attending them in their Yorkshire castles, still retain three in their service in Northumberland (I, xxxiii; xxxv–xxxvi; lxxiii–lxxv).

Percy's changes in three of his essays are comparatively minor.[39] To the fourth, the "Essay on the Ancient English Minstrels." he felt compelled to give major attention. In a paper read at a meeting of the Society of Antiquaries on May 29, 1766, the antiquarian Samuel Pegge expressed the view that Percy in his essay had given "a false, or at best, an ill-grounded idea" of the "rank and condition" of the minstrels in Saxon times.[40] Pegge argued that the customs of ancient Britons and Danes were too different from those of the Saxons to conclude, as Percy does, that, because the Britons and Danes accorded a high place to their bards and scalds, the Saxons would have done the same with their own minstrels. He went on to cast doubt upon two stories recounted by Percy to exemplify the Saxons's esteem for their minstrels, one of King Alfred assuming the dress and character of a minstrel in order to gain admittance to the Danish camp, and the other of the Danish King Anlaff employing the same ruse to gain admittance among the Saxons. The first he thought of doubtful authority, and the second probably adapted from it.

It is a revealing commentary upon Percy that his most extensive revision for the second edition should have been undertaken as a result of a paper read before a meeting of antiquarians and written by a man scarcely known outside of antiquarian circles. Percy was not present at the Society's May 29 meeting, but was sent a copy of Pegge's paper by Sir Joseph Ayloffe, and he was clearly annoyed that Pegge had not favored *him* with his objections rather than forcing him to rely upon a third person to convey them to him. As a result, he wrote to Pegge on July 13, 1767, he might have remained ignorant of them and thus incapable of retracting his errors.[41] Scholar that he was, Percy cared very much about his standing among fellow scholars.

Percy did not acknowledge his debt to Pegge's paper until the third edition of the *Reliques* in 1775, but readers of the second edition familiar with Pegge's comments could not have mistaken Percy's intentions. Percy, to be sure, does not confess to error, and when he finishes his revision for the 1767 edition his position is essentially what it was in 1765. But he is plainly acknowledging the justice of Pegge's assertion that he had given at best "an ill-grounded idea" of the rank and condition of the Saxon minstrels, for the whole intent of his effort is to establish his position on firmer ground.

The initial essay was nine pages long. The revised essay contains twenty pages. In 1765 the comments about the Anglo-Saxon minstrels, culminating in the stories of Alfred and Anlaff, fill the first three pages of the essay, with Percy stating categorically at the beginning that "Our Saxon ancestors ... had been accustomed to hold men of this profession in the highest reverence" (I, xv). In 1767 he withholds any word about the Anglo-Saxons until he is midway into the second page, his introductory page and a half having been directed toward justifying a more cautious assertion: "As these honours were paid to Poetry and Song, from the earliest times, in those countries which our Anglo-Saxon ancestors inhabited before their removal into Britain, we may reasonably conclude, that they would not lay aside all their regard for men of this sort immediately on quitting their German forests"(I, xx). If, moreover, bards were revered in the countries inhabited by the Anglo-Saxons before they removed to Britain, and were "common and numerous" among descendants of the Anglo-Saxons in Britain after the Conquest, what, asks Percy, "could have become of them in the intermediate time?" He sees no alternative to concluding that the minstrels still subsisted, "though perhaps with less splendour" than in Northern Europe. "and that there never was wanting a succession of them to hand down the art "(I, xxiii). He then repeats his stories of Alfred and Anlaff, adds a third story to them, defends his au-

thorities, and insists upon the spirit of the stories if not the
letter: "they are related by authors who lived too near the Saxon
times, and had before them too many recent monuments of the
Anglo-Saxon nation, not to know what was conformable to the
genius and manners of that people" (I, xxiii–xxvi).

The revised account, in short, was fuller and more carefully
reasoned than the original, and Percy also took the opportunity
to inject into it some of the history of the minstrels between the
Conquest and the reign of Edward II, a period he had ignored
in the first edition. But the response to Pegge was still not finished
when Percy had revised the text of the essay. The original had
been footnoted unobtrusively, and the revised essay is footnoted
with similar restraint, with the notes indicated by the customary
asterisks, daggers, and crosses of the period. There is, however,
a second system of reference marks in the revised essay which
begins with A and proceeds through the alphabet and into a
second alphabet to *Ff*. The letters are placed before the first
words of paragraphs, and the notes to which they refer are
printed at the end of the essay. The notes fill thirty-eight pages,
almost twice as many, that is, as the revised essay itself. No such
notes had been attached to the 1765 essay.

What Percy collects in these notes may be considered relevant
to his essay, and much of it is interesting. He draws upon a wide
variety of sources, including the Anglo-Saxon language, for such
purposes as suggesting the likelihood that King Alfred excelled
in music, describing the roles of the minstrels, demonstrating
in response to a challenge by Pegge that the Anglo-Saxons had
a word for minstrelsy, and above all supporting his thesis that
they held both music and musicians in high regard. But what
was relevant was not necessarily essential, and what was interesting in its parts was by no means interesting in the whole.
Indeed, the conclusion is inescapable that in these thirty-eight
pages Percy abandoned his chosen role as an editor seeking to
please a general audience and was now the scholar addressing
other scholars. What Shenstone feared and had counseled Percy
against had happened. Readers who had enjoyed Percy's essay,
and who would go on to delight in the songs and ballads that
he spread before them, could only have turned with distaste
from the "Notes and Illustrations Referred to in the Foregoing

Essay." Its long, untranslated quotations in Latin, French, and
Spanish stretched like roadblocks across a dozen and a half pages,
while its five-page disquisition on the Anglo-Saxon language
would have seemed better suited for a gathering at the Society
of Antiquaries.

Percy's reaction to Pegge's criticism serves as a graphic reminder of his dilemma in editing the *Reliques*, as well as of
Shenstone's influence in shaping the *Reliques* into the landmark
it became. The scholar in Percy impelled him to prop up his
sagging essay with notes and references which would withstand
further criticism. As for Shenstone, it is hard to imagine that he
could have objected to the revised essay, which was clearly
superior to the original; but surely if he had lived to see the
thirty-eight pages of notes he would have thrown up his hands
and urged Percy to communicate them to Pegge and the scholarly
world in some other form. It would have been good advice, and
it would probably have been taken.

In spite of their unpromising introduction, Percy and Pegge
became good friends. In occasional letters Pegge answered
Percy's inquiries on antiquarian matters, and Percy presented
Pegge with copies of the *Ride to Hulne Abbey* and the *Northumberland Houshold Book*. Thus both seemed distressed in 1773
when the Society of Antiquaries published Pegge's 1766 observations in the second volume of *Archaeologia*; and Pegge wrote
to Percy promptly to say that the Council of the Society was
apparently unaware that Percy had responded to his objections
in the 1767 *Reliques* and to state formally that Percy had removed
his doubts "in a very satisfactory manner."[42] In the 1775 *Reliques*
Percy announced that since the first edition the essay had been
"very much enlarged and improved" as a result of Pegge's objections, which Pegge, "in the most liberal and candid manner,"
now acknowledged to have been removed (I, xviii).

V *The Ritson Controversy and the Fourth Edition*

The controversy with Samuel Pegge, if it can be called a
controversy, was settled amicably and fairly quickly, although
not without Percy's going to an extraordinary effort to satisfy
Pegge's objections. A controversy of a different sort, far from

being settled quickly and amicably, was never settled at all, and it was much more serious in its implications and consequences.

It had its beginnings in a three-volume publication of 1783 entitled *A Select Collection of English Songs*, which was compiled by Joseph Ritson. Ritson, who became a solicitor of Gray's Inn, was an accomplished and brilliant scholar, but stormy and eccentric. His aggressive vegetarianism, along with his efforts to reform English spelling, provided considerable amusement for his contemporaries—a collection which he published in 1802 was entitled *Ancient Engleish Metrical Romanceës*—and his attacks upon other scholars resounded with an explosive mixture of irony, sarcasm, and invective that made him a feared and at times a hated controversialist. Alexander Chalmers, in a wry defense, noted that Ritson was "not absolutely incapable of civility."[43] He was to pursue Percy, with occasional lapses into civility, until his death in 1803 at the age of fifty-one.

In *A Select Collection of English Songs*, Ritson praised Percy's translation of "Rio Verde, Rio Verde" and printed "O Nancy, Wilt Thou Go with Me" among the large group of love songs in his first volume; a "most beautiful song," he called it.[44] But Ritson's attention, like Pegge's before him, was drawn primarily to Percy's "Essay on the Ancient English Minstrels," which he considered in his own "Historical Essay on the Origin and Progress of National Song." While not attempting to controvert "the slightest fact laid down by the learned prelate," Ritson wrote, he thought that he might be permitted "to question the propriety of his inferences, and, indeed, his general hypothesis." It does not follow, he argues, that because the French honored the minstrels the English must have done so also; nor is there any proof that the English minstrels were "a respectable society" or that they deserved to be called a society at all:

That there were men in those times, as there are in the present, who gained a livelihood by going about from place to place, singing and playing to the illiterate vulgar, is doubtless true; but that they were received into the castles of the nobility, sung at their tables, and were rewarded like the French minstrels, does not any where appear, nor is it at all credible. (I, li–lii)

The reason, says Ritson, is evident. At least till the time of Henry VIII only the French language was spoken at court and in the households of the Norman barons, who despised the Saxon manners and language. Percy's essay should properly have been called an "Essay on the Ancient FRENCH Minstrels," for all that is known of the English is that by a law of Queen Elizabeth's time they were branded as "rogues, vagabonds, and sturdy beggars." Such characters could "sing and play; but it was none of their business to read or write"; thus their songs have perished along with them, and only "The Ancient Ballad of Chevy-Chase" and "The Battle of Otterbourne" can be ascribed with any plausibility to them (I, liii).

Ritson returned to this subject in *Ancient Songs, from the Time of King Henry the Third, to the Revolution,* which was published in 1790. In his 26-page "Observations on the Ancient English Minstrels," he attacks Percy's definition of the minstrel. This order of men who, he says (mocking Percy's words), "united the arts of poetry and music, and sung verses to the harp of their own composing," had in fact little more standing than the whores and lechers "for whose diversion . . . [they] were most miserably twanging and scraping in the booths of Chester fair" (vi–vii). Before Percy, he asserts, the word "minstrel" was never used by an English writer for anyone but an instrumental performer, "generally a fiddler, or such like base musician." No English minstrel "was ever famous for his composition or his performance; nor is the name of a single one preserved" (xiii, xvi).

Ritson then moved to his more significant attack upon Percy— one which he had begun in *A Select Collection of English Songs* —by noting that, of the black-letter ballads he had himself collated, not one had been printed faithfully or correctly by Percy. Percy's editorial practices now became his essential focus, and he was to return to them again and again during the remaining years of his life.

He begins by doubting the very existence of Percy's folio manuscript: since the minstrels never committed their own rhymes to writing, it is extraordinary that this "multifarious collection" could have been compiled as late as 1650. And, to increase the manuscript's singularity, "no other writer has ever pretended to have seen [it]. The late Mr. Tyrwhitt . . . never saw it. . . . And it is remarkable, that scarcely any thing is published from it, not being to be found elsewhere, without our being told of the defects and mutilation of the MS" (xix). He then cites seven poems printed by Percy from the folio manuscript—"Sir Cauline," "Sir Aldingar," "Gentle Herdsman," "The Heir of Linne," "The Beggar's Daughter of Bednall-Green," "The Marriage of Sir Gawaine," and "King Arthur's Death"—in which Percy acknowledged his emendations largely in general terms, and he states that many "other instances might be noticed, where the learned collector has preferred his ingenuity to his fidelity, without the least intimation to the reader." It follows, asserts Ritson, that one can have no confidence in any of the *Reliques*'s "old Minstrel ballads" which cannot be found elsewhere (xx–xxi).

The minstrels, Ritson notes, lost favor to the ballad singers, who, without instruments, sung printed pieces to fine and simple melodies, possibly of their own invention," and whose verses, smoother in language than the minstrel poems and more accurate in measure and rhyme, were thought to be more poetical; and in fact (a view which Percy and later ballad scholars did not share with Ritson) they may "defy all the Minstrel songs extant, nay even those in the *Reliques of Ancient English Poetry,* for simplicity, nature, interest, and pathos." The minstrel songs are "curious and valuable," nonetheless, and if further light could be thrown on the people by or for whom they were "invented," a collection of all the available poems would be entertaining and interesting. But, he adds, with a final thrust at Percy, "if such a publication should ever appear, it is to be hoped that it will come from an Editor who prefers truth to hypothesis, and the genuine remains of the Minstrel Poets, however mutilated or rude, to the indulgence of his own poetical vein, however fluent or refined" (xxvi).

As early as the spring of 1784, James Dodsley inquired if Percy wished to supply copy for a fourth edition of the *Reliques.*[45] By then, of course, Percy was in Northern Ireland serving as bishop of Dromore, and, however he may have responded in 1784, he apparently wrote to Dodsley on November 19, 1785, to say that it was a matter of "perfect Indifference" to him whether the *Reliques* was ever republished or not. He would be glad to have it forgotten "among the other Levities & Vanities" of his youth, as he had concluded from an earlier Dodsley letter would be its fate. He was thus unprepared to send corrected copy immediately, and he left it to Dodsley either to consign the book to oblivion or to give him more time.[46]

As might have been expected, Dodsley chose the second of these alternatives, but no record of further negotiations remains. In its issue of July 8–10, 1794, the *St. James's Chronicle* announced that the fourth edition would "Speedily" be published, and though the three volumes bear the date 1794 a full year seems to have passed before they were actually made available to the public.[47] They were printed by Percy's friend and kinsman John Nichols and published by J. and C. Rivington rather than by Dodsley, who had retired from business.

In the "Advertisement" at the front of the fourth edition, which is signed by Percy's nephew Thomas Percy of St. John's College, Oxford, it is stated that the book would have remained unpublished had "the original Editor ... not yielded to the importunity of his friends, and accepted the humble offer of an Editor in a Nephew" (I, ix). It is doubtful if anyone who has studied the *Reliques* has given much credence to that statement. Well paid though Percy's nephew was for whatever services he rendered,[48] his designation as editor of the fourth edition was almost certainly a polite fiction intended to mask the fact that the bishop of Dromore was publicly exposing the "Levities and Vanities" of his youth. Percy was later to take his nephew to task for revealing to George Steevens (of all people!) that he was only an "umbra" in the edition, a choice bit of news that the mischievous Steevens did not scruple to pass on to Ritson.[49] It seems a safe assumption also that Percy would not have entrusted the writing of a rather sensitive "Advertisement" to a nephew whose "Tastes & Persuits," as Percy wrote to his wife on September 17, 1799, "are so different from mine."[60] It is hard to think of anything else in the three volumes that might be claimed for the younger Thomas Percy.

Friends may have urged a new edition upon Percy, but in all likelihood the chief incentive for revising the third edition was to respond to Ritson's attack in *Ancient Songs* upon his integrity and method. Probably he could have passed over Ritson's strictures on the "Essay on the Ancient English Minstrels" in *A Select*

Collection of English Songs, if only from the sheer weariness of having revised the essay once before. But Percy was not one to receive with equanimity the suggestion that his folio manuscript was a fabrication, like Chatterton's Rowley or Macpherson's Ossian poems. And one may suppose that, once he had decided upon the task of revision, the scholar in him would simply not permit him to ignore what Ritson had to say about the minstrels and leave his essay untouched. The result of this two-fold approach to the fourth edition was that the changes in it, if not numerous, were significant, and that nearly all of them can be traced to one or the other of the two Ritson works.

The opening "Advertisement" is itself a key part of Percy's response: "The appeal publicly made to Dr. JOHNSON . . . [in the 1765 preface], and never once contradicted by him during so large a portion of his life, ought to have precluded every doubt concerning the existence of the MS. in question." But because a doubt was expressed, the manuscript was left for a year at the home of John Nichols, where it was examined "by many Gentlemen of eminence in literature" (I, x). Much of the rest of the "Advertisement" describes the manuscript, with emphasis upon its missing leaves and parts of leaves and its faulty transcriptions often made from defective copies, with the result that "a considerable portion of the song or narrative is sometimes omitted; and miserable trash or nonsense not unfrequently introduced into pieces of considerable merit" (I, xii). In a few paragraphs, in short, Ritson's intolerable implication is disposed of and a basis for Percy's editorial practice established.

The "Advertisement" was new to the fourth edition. Of the continuing parts of the text, Percy once again undertook a major revision of the "Essay on the Ancient English Minstrels." Already doubled in size to meet Samuel Pegge's objections, it was now increased by another two thirds, and its unsightly supplementary notes were swollen from thirty-eight pages to fifty-two. Percy's purpose is to make clear, first, that such a person as the *English* minstrel did in fact survive the Conquest and, second, that he was welcomed in the houses of leading English families. Drawing upon the histories of music published by Sir John Hawkins and Charles Burney in 1776, he progresses from the reign of Henry I to the reign of Elizabeth, filling in some of the gaps in the royal succession he had left in earlier editions and citing, when he can, both the names of minstrels and the honors accorded them. He acknowledges that "in the first ages after the Conquest no other songs would be listened to by the great nobility" than those composed in the Norman French (I, xxix–xxx). But the Anglo-Saxons, although they now occupied inferior positions, were not "extirpated," and they could understand only their own gleemen or minstrels—bards, harpers, even dancers and mimics—who were readily admitted into the households of the English gentry (I, xxx).

Thus, accepting Ritson's conclusions in part, Percy relegates the English minstrels to a position below that of the French but reputable nonetheless; and he follows the two lines of their histories as they are gradually drawn together while the French and English cultures in Britain blend into one. The result is both a fuller essay and a more discriminating one. It is not likely, of course, that Percy hoped to satisfy Ritson's doubts as he had satisfied Samuel Pegge's in 1767. Percy and Pegge were much closer in spirit, apostles of a politer form of scholarly controversy than Ritson ever pretended to. It was not impossible, on the other hand, that, satisfied or not, Ritson would call off his pursuit of Percy's essay. That he would cease his attacks upon Percy's editorial practices was hardly to be expected. Percy trusted Ritson so little, in fact, that he gave express orders that he was not to be shown the folio manuscript while it was on display at the home of John Nichols.[51] From other scholars Percy had reason to expect a sympathetic response. To grant Ritson access to the manuscript was to place a battery of cannon at his disposal with the likelihood that he would discharge it triumphantly in Percy's face at the first opportunity.

For Percy was well aware that editorially in the *Reliques* he and Ritson were in opposing and irreconcilable camps. The difficulty of Percy's position was that, being a scholar himself, he could appreciate Ritson's concern for accurate texts of the poems, whereas he saw not the slightest chance that Ritson would appreciate his decision to subordinate textual accuracy to the desire to appeal to a broad spectrum of readers. It had been Shenstone's view that there were a good many encumbrances to the old poems which had to be shaken loose if the collection was to be a success, and Percy had agreed, although not without that lingering regret that scholars are likely to feel when they yield to the impulse to popularize. His hope, of course, was to have the best of both the scholarly and popular worlds. Scholars, including Ritson, were unfailingly impressed by the imagination and erudition that went into the *Reliques*, but in this instance Percy's sheer abilities had the consequence, at least with a fellow scholar of Ritson's caliber and temperament, of throwing his unscholarly editorial practices into sharp relief. A lesser man than Percy might have been ignored or at least more readily forgiven. If he was not, he might simply have charged Ritson with pedantry and counted upon his nonscholar readers to support him. But that course was not open to Percy. Ultimately the "improvements" that he subjected many of the poems to could be justified only on the ground of the book's success, and that was the ground that Percy chose.

The public, concludes the fourth edition "Advertisement" ostensibly written by Percy's nephew,

may judge how much they are indebted to the composer of this collection; who, at an early period of life, with such materials and such subjects, formed a work which hath been admitted into the most elegant libraries; and with which the judicious Antiquary hath just reason to be satisfied, while refined entertainment hath been provided for every Reader of taste and genius. (I, xii)

Few of Percy's contemporaries would have thought the claim extravagant. The sale of three good-sized editions, the first and third of 1,500 copies[52] and probably the second also, was an achievement for a three-volume work of collected poetry in the late eighteenth century. For a collection largely of old ballads it was phenomenal, and until the publication of Walter Scott's *Minstrelsy of the Scottish Border* in 1802 no other collection began to approach the *Reliques* in popularity. Ritson's collections of accurately printed texts seem not to have captured the public's fancy at all.

A significant part of Percy's defense was the need to repair the damage suffered by many of the poems, some of which were missing whole sections. To have printed them as they were

would have satisfied the desire for scholarly accuracy; but
Shenstone and Percy were persuaded that it would turn away
many of the very readers they were hoping to attract. The alternatives were not to print them at all or to print them with
such interpolations or additions as Percy thought appropriate.
He chose the second alternative.

Had he confined his efforts to those poems which, as he
viewed them, could benefit from minor repairs, he would doubtless have been spared the full fury of later scholars when the
folio manuscript was finally published by John W. Hales and
Frederick J. Furnivall in 1867 and 1868. Smoothing the meter
of the old verses and modifying the diction or the rhyme, along
with such changes in punctuation, capitalization, and spelling
as were commonplace among editors, might at times have been
justified by the need to clarify the poems for eighteenth-century
readers, whose knowledge of the old poetic vocabulary was
minuscule. And even in a more extensively amended poem like
"Gentle Herdsman, Tell to Me," Percy's additions were not likely
to seem a serious disturbance, filling in conjecturally as they do
a series of gaps in this unique copy of the poem. They appear
in a sequence of thirteen lines toward the middle of the poem's
sixty lines, with Percy's interpolations designated by his own
italics:

> I am a woman, woe is me!
>   *Born* to greeffe and irksome care.
>
> *For* my beloved, and well-beloved,
>   *My wayward cruelty could kill:*
> *And though my teares will nought avail,*
>   *Most dearely I bewail him* still.
>
> *He was the flower of* noble wights,
>   *None ever more sincere colde* bee;
> *Of comely mien and shape* he was,
>   *And tenderlye hee* loved mee.
>
> *When thus I saw he lov*ed me well,
>   *I grewe so proud his pai*ne to see,

> *That I, who did not* know myselfe,
> *Thought scorne of such a youth* as hee.
>
> (II, 73–74)

It cannot be said that Percy's invention rose to the challenge of these ragged verses. Most of his lines are banal at best, and *sincere* was an utter stranger to the ballad vocabulary. But Furnivall's comment in *Bishop Percy's Folio Manuscript* seems rather too harsh for the offense: "We are not quite sure that the hand of time was always more to be dreaded than the hand of the Bishop" (III, 526). Even Ritson did not object to Percy's practice with "Gentle Herdsman," although he was unable to resist commenting that the poem "has not the least appearance of being a Minstrel Song" (*Ancient Songs*, p. xx).

In the various prefaces to the poems cited by Ritson, Percy noted that his texts included "conjectural emendations" and even wholly rewritten or additional stanzas and sections. What he failed to do was to follow his practice in "Gentle Herdsman" and point out precisely the extent and location of his alterations. With "The Beggar's Daughter of Bednall-Green," for example, he stated that "the concluding stanzas, which contain the old Beggar's discovery of himself," are "a modern attempt to remove the absurdities and inconsistencies ... of the song, as it stood before" (4th ed., II, 162), but that information still left the reader with some doubt as to which stanzas he had altered. As for "The Marriage of Sir Gawaine," to cite another example from the seven poems, Percy had stated from the beginning that half of each manuscript leaf had been torn away and that he would in time print the truncated original text so that readers might compare it with his own interpolated version. With all these poems, of course, one could wish that Percy had found a convenient way to call attention both to his specific changes and to the originals, but it would be incorrect to conclude that he failed to inform his readers that he had taken liberties with his texts.

Considering the extent of Percy's changes, one can imagine the cry that Ritson would have sent up if he had been granted access to the folio manuscript. For some of Percy's "conjectural emendations" virtually obscured the manuscripts they were

emendating. "The Child of Elle," for example, a mere thirty-
nine lines in Percy's folio, grew to a strapping two hundred in
the *Reliques*, while "Sir Cauline" nearly doubled its size from
201 to 392. "The Child of Elle" was an unprintable if unique
fragment, however, without beginning or end but with enough
apparent merit to stir the poet in Percy to "a strong desire to
attempt a completion of the story" (I, 90). Indeed, Percy's only
real offense in this instance was in not proving a better poet.
With regard to "Sir Cauline" and some of the other poems, the
controversy has been more substantial. Percy found his manuscript copy of "Sir Cauline" "so very defective and mutilated"
that he added "several stanzas in the first part, and still more
in the second, to connect and compleat the story in the manner
which appeared to him most interesting and affecting" (4th ed.,
I, 41). Hales, letting Percy off comparatively lightly, remarked
that Percy's version abounds in affectations and expressed a
preference for the folio copy, "with all its roughness and imper-
fections."[53] Wheatley, less forgiving, saw "no necessity for this
perversion of the original, because the story is . . . complete"
(I, 62). Hales's indictment is of the poet; Wheatley's, of the
editor. But sometimes with Percy the two roles merge, as they
do in "Sir Cauline." If Percy found the temptation to experiment
with his poems simply overwhelming at times, he also found
support for that activity in one of his guiding principles: considerable license might be permitted an editor whose texts
were not to be trusted—"copied from the faulty recitation of
some illiterate minstrell," as he wrote of "Sir Cauline" in the
fourth edition (I, 41).

This was not an easy position to carry in debate, however,
and no doubt Percy was aware that he had stretched the principle pretty far in a few of the poems. Perhaps those facts account
for his not replying to Ritson's criticisms with a detailed defense
of specific alterations. On the other hand, he did not ignore
them. He printed the folio manuscript fragment of "The Marriage of Sir Gawaine" at the end of the fourth edition and thus
belatedly fulfilled a first edition promise (I, 11). He did not
modify his texts of the seven poems cited by Ritson or provide
any precise index of his revisions, but he placed three asterisks
at the end of the forty-eight poems in which "any considerable

liberties were taken with the old copies" (4th ed., I, xvii). Except for the "Essay on the Ancient English Minstrels," his changes in the fourth edition are, in fact, comparatively few, and, like those in the essay, most of them were obviously stimulated by Ritson's criticism. A good many relate to his use of the folio manuscript. They include a number of additional footnotes citing divergences from the manuscript, some additional introductory acknowledgments of Percy's changes in the poems, a reversion in the title of "The Wandering Prince of Troy" to the folio manuscript title "Queen Dido," and a note appended to "The Heir of Linne" indicating that "several ancient readings are restored from the folio MS." In the introduction to "Old Robin of Portingale," Percy announces that he is now dropping Robin's title of "Sir" because he is called only Robin in the manuscript; and in "A Lover of Late" he quietly corrects his only significant departure from the text by replacing "fond" in line seventeen with the manuscript's word "kind": "I was as kind as she was faire."[54]

Percy and Ritson were never reconciled either personally or professionally, and it cannot be said that their hostility brought out the best in either. In 1802 Ritson attacked Percy with particular fury in *Ancient Engleish Metrical Romanceës*, where he accused him of practicing "every kind of forgery and imposture" (cxliii, n.). As for Percy, he provided his friend Robert Nares with three paragraphs supplementary to Nares's review of *Ancient Engleish Metrical Romanceës* in the December, 1804, *British Critic*, of which Nares was editor, and Nares printed them separately in the January, 1805, issue as a "Supplemental Article" submitted by a "friend" of Percy.[55] Percy also secured an account of an incident shortly before Ritson's death in September, 1803, in which Ritson set fire to his manuscripts in his chambers in Gray's Inn and, when challenged respecting his behavior, replied that he was writing a pamphlet proving Christ to have been an impostor. Robert Anderson, to whom Percy sent a copy of the account, informed him in a letter of June 22, 1811, that it had been published in Cromek's *Select Scotish Songs*.[56]

If not already of that opinion, Percy—"the worthy and venerable Bishop of Dromore," as the *British Critic* called him—must have been convinced by the Gray's Inn incident that Ritson was quite insane, and perhaps it is not surprising that he took some pains to have the strange conduct of his severest critic made known. It would have been better, of course, for him to ignore Ritson's continuing attacks upon him. His reputation was secure, at least for his own time, and in his final edition of the *Reliques* he had put forth the best defense of his practices that he knew and had again shown himself ready to acknowledge criticism with careful self-examination. The excellent fourth edition of the *Reliques* was the high point of an extraordinary scholarly career, and it was itself the most persuasive argument in support of Percy's case.

CHAPTER 5

Later Years

ALTHOUGH Johnson, Shenstone, Grainger, and others had recognized his promise, Percy can be said to have begun the decade of the 1760s as a virtual unknown. A mere occasional contributor to the *Grand Magazine,* the *Universal Visiter,* and *The Library*—even a poet enshrined in Dodsley's *Collection*— might pass unnoticed by all but his closest friends. By 1771, however, Percy had written or edited ten books and seen the *Reliques* through a revised second edition, and he had thus assured himself a welcome in literary circles everywhere. He was, in fact, well on his way to becoming a household name both in Britain and on the Continent.

Had other duties not distracted him, Percy might have attempted to repeat the success of those early years. With adequate time to devote to them, he might have spared the editions of Surrey and Buckingham their fiery deaths in John Nichols's warehouse and preserved the *Tatler, Spectator,* and *Guardian* for his own editorship rather than John Calder's. His mind fairly teemed with projects. Adding a fourth volume to the *Reliques* was always of interest to him, and he drew up any number of plans for new collections of ancient poetry, only to file them away at last among the voluminous archives that he bequeathed to his family. He collected materials for an edition of *Don Quixote,* and he brought *Ancient Songs Chiefly on Moorish Subjects* to the point of publication before he abandoned it.

Thus no second miraculous decade followed the first. No doubt Percy was to some extent a victim of his own innumerable literary interests; they might have fared better if he had taken them in succession rather than virtually all at once. But Percy's curiosity was not easily confined to narrow channels, and his success in the decade of the sixties had fully vindicated his practice of giving almost simultaneous attention to multiple projects. Clearly his most serious obstacle in the seventies was the steadily dwindling leisure which was the penalty of success. Literary friends and correspondences had to be cultivated. Even more obviously, Percy's clerical duties were mounting. The earl of Sussex's chaplain became the duke of Northumberland's chaplain also, and then in 1769 a chaplain in ordinary to the king as well. To the duke he was also a secretary, and to members of the duke's family an increasing confidant and friend. He kept in touch with the duchess while she traveled on the Continent from 1767 to 1769,[1] and some years later he cheered Lord Percy with news from home when the young lord, a major general and later a lieutenant general, was commanding British troops in the effort to suppress the American rebellion.[2] With his appointment as dean of Carlisle in 1778 and then as bishop of Dromore in 1782, any chance that Percy might resume a literary activity even remotely comparable to that of the 1760s was irrevocably lost.

This is not to suggest that Percy's pen was idle during the last thirty or forty years of his life. Calls for a third and then a fourth edition of the *Reliques*, as we have seen, drew him back to the ballads in time for publication in 1775 and 1795. The *Key to the New Testament* benefited from his occasional revisions. The editions of Surrey and Buckingham endured an all but incredible gestation period of forty-five years, only to perish almost as the midwife was at hand. Minor antiquarian works, notes on Shakespeare and Johnson, occasional reviews, comments on literary figures, a substantial biographical article and a more substantial memoir—if these seem only a modest sequel to the *Reliques of Ancient English Poetry,* they may on the other hand be counted a creditable performance for a conscientious divine whose primary duties were as dean of Carlisle and bishop of Dromore.

I *Minor Works*

Much of Percy's writing during his last years was inconsequential, a kind of hurried ephemera born out of his own irrepressible curiosity and the pleasure of sharing his knowledge with others. Even scientific inquiry (as Percy may have thought of it) attracted him from time to time. A 1783 letter to Michael Lort in which Percy recorded his purchase of "a pair of the largest fossil horns, I believe, ever found in Ireland," was read at the Society of Antiquaries on December 4, 1783, and published in *Archaeologia* in 1785.[3] A letter on "Swallows, Cuckoos, and Falling Stones" became the lead article of the March, 1797, *Gentleman's Magazine,* Percy's contribution to resolving the mysteries of bird migration, with an added speculation that stones sometimes fall from the clouds because lightning may strike a rock with such force as to hurl a fragment "through the air, at a distance of a few miles."[4] In January, 1805, Percy supplied the *Gentleman's Magazine* with a testimony to the efficacy of brown paper in curing rheumatism.[5] A Mrs. K—— of Oxford Street, he noted, "was cured of rheumatic pains in a few days by wearing a waistcoat of brown paper," and he had heard that Sir Wm. P "applied it by only covering the ears, and was cured of a deafness." He himself, he confessed, had "used the common brown paper, which is made of junk (old rope); it smells of tar, and it is best to rub it smooth with a black glass bottle." A fascination with old rope, of course, was hardly more becoming to a bishop than a predilection for old ballads, and it is understandable that Percy would conceal his identity by subscribing only the initials B. D. (bishop of Dromore?) to his letter.

The May, 1802, *Gentleman's Magazine* contains a brief memorial of the recently deceased physician James Johnstone which was apparently written by Percy, who would have taken a natural interest in Johnstone because of their common connections with Worcester and Samuel Johnson.[6] The May issue's lead article, an essay on the Giant's Causeway written by W. R. and originally published in the Belfast and Dublin newspapers, contains a preface signed A. B. and probably written by Percy, along with an introductory note certainly by Percy, who received an acknowledgment of the materials in a May 31 letter from John Nichols.[7]

In the preface A. B. called attention to a painting of the Giant's Causeway by Thomas Robinson which would be "disposed of by raffle to one hundred subscribers at one guinea each," as Robinson's painting of the Battle of Ballynahinch had been sold after the Irish rebellion of 1798. Robinson, who had

studied under George Romney, painted portraits of the Percy
children and grandchildren, and his son Thomas Romney Robinson was a literary prodigy of whom Percy was very fond. The
Gentleman's Magazine, perhaps on Percy's recommendation, had
begun publishing young Robinson's poetry in 1801 when he was
only eight years old. In 1803 Percy forwarded two additional
Robinson poems with a request that John Nichols "take off" two
dozen copies and send them to him in Ireland,[8] and in 1805
he submitted the "Infant Bard's" "Verses on the Death of William
Cunningham" with his own letter on the uses of brown paper.[9]
The next year saw the publication of a subscription volume
entitled *Juvenile Poems* and dedicated to Percy, who subscribed
to forty copies and his wife to ten.[10] The volume, understandably
enough, is a testimonial to Robinson's precocity rather than to
his genius, but, with the lieutenant governor of Ireland (the earl
of Hardwicke) heading the list of subscribers with sixty-three
copies and the bishop of Dromore not far behind with forty,
perhaps it is not surprising that national pride could be stirred
to a subscription list for these infant rhapsodies to the extent of
1,414 names and 2,064 copies.[11]

Authors old and young engaged Percy's attention in his Dromore years. In the 1790 *Gentleman's Magazine* he defended the
memory of Jonathan Swift against a charge in the new *Tatler*
edition that Swift had once committed a rape,[12] and in the same
magazine for 1802 (8) he answered the inquiry of a correspon-
dent by citing an obscure edition of Shakespeare's poems published by Thomas Cotes. He undertook a more extensive effort
in 1801, when he reviewed Jane West's *Letters Addressed to a
Young Man* in a nineteen-page article, most of it quotations
from the book, spread over the issues of the *British Critic* for
September, October, and November.[13] Percy praised Mrs. West
for her "orthodox, temperate, uniform, and liberal" doctrines,
and for recommending manners that "every judicious parent
would wish a son to adopt" (September, p. 287). He welcomed
also Mrs. West's "determined resistance to ... pestiferous doctrines" like the "sentimental wickedness" of Goethe and Rous-
seau, and he commended her for examining "those democratical
notions which affect government, property, and the origin of
society" and for sustaining her former character "as a lover of

order, subordination, and lawful authority" (November, pp. 526–27).

If to modern ears Percy's comments sound anomalous for the year 1801, they serve nonetheless as a useful reminder that the old views were not entirely dislodged by the American and French Revolutions and a new generation of poets and philosophers. Like many of his contemporaries, Percy carried convictions into the nineteenth century that he had shared with Johnson and other spokesmen of the mid- and late eighteenth century, and he rejected categorically what he referred to as "the new philosophy" (September, p. 287). Mrs. West, with whom he corresponded from 1800 until his death, was one of the old school and worthy for that reason to be encouraged. But doubtless he was pleased to support her also because, as he noted at the end of his review, she was a Northamptonshire native. For Percy the ties of blood and place were uncommonly strong, and they are reflected in a number of his lesser works. His attempt at a history of the house of Percy has already been mentioned, along with his other literary efforts for his Northumberland patron. An account of Lindridge and a Lowe-Percy genealogy prepared for Treadway Nash's *History and Antiquities of Worcestershire*, for all the drudgery they required of him, were labors of love, as were his slighter contributions to John Nichols's *History and Antiquities of Hinckley* and *History and Antiquities of the County of Leicester*, the county of Mrs. Percy and the Gutteridge family.[14] Percy reviewed the third volume, part 1, of Nichols's history of Leicestershire for the *British Critic* in October, 1800 (345–61) and under cover of his anonymity took the occasion to cite the history's defense of his brother-in-law William Gutteridge's action in removing an ancient Roman milestone from the roadside at Thurmaston.

Family connection induced a special pride in Percy, and almost none gave him more pleasure than that with the seventeenth-century poet John Cleiveland, a brother of Percy's great-grandfather. Cleiveland's name comes up frequently in his correspondence with his cousin William Cleiveland, whose relationship with the poet was identical with Percy's; and Percy was delighted to be able to purchase a portrait of the poet during the sale of James West's effects on April 3, 1773. James Boswell,

who visited Percy at Northumberland House on April 7, was
treated to a view of the picture and to an account of some of
Percy's "active schemes of curious and amusing literature."[15]

A scheme probably not yet active but perhaps under consideration was a memoir of the poet Cleiveland. It did not appear
until 1784, however, when it was published in volume 3 of the
Biographia Britannica's second edition.[16] Most of its five folio
pages are biographical rather than critical, and its footnotes,
which include a long extract from Cleiveland's "The Rebel Scot"
and a letter to Cromwell with which Cleiveland secured his
release from prison, occupy more than twice as much space as
the text. By and large, both text and notes are drily factual, but
the final paragraph is of interest for its general assessment of
Cleiveland's achievement as a poet. Warmly partisan as he was,
Percy might have been expected to lavish praise upon this illus-
trious brother of his great-grandfather. Instead he begins his
evaluation by allying Cleiveland with those poets who, as Johnson wrote in his *Life of Cowley,* paid "their court to temporary
prejudices, [and thus] have been at one time too much praised,
and at another too much neglected." Cleiveland excelled, Percy
notes, among those metaphysical poets who "abound with
witty rather than just thoughts, with far-fetched conceits, and
learned allusions, that only amuse for a moment, utterly neglect-
ing that beautiful simplicity and propriety, which will interest
and please through every age." Yet in his time he was preferred
before Milton, whose "works could, with difficulty, gain admission to the press": "But Cleiveland is now sunk into oblivion,
while Milton's fame is universally diffused . . . . The press now
continually teems with re-publications of the Paradise Lost, &c.
whereas the last edition of Cleiveland's works was in 8vo. 1687."

Having argued with such conviction that Cleiveland was too
much praised in his own day, Percy has nothing left to support
an argument that he was subsequently too much neglected; for
one can only wonder how a poet utterly unmindful of simplicity
and propriety—who abounds with witty rather than just thoughts
—can possibly have sufficient appeal to warrant the tribute of
republication. It is almost as though Percy, having sensed the
folly of trying to revive John Cleiveland's reputation, is lashing
the poet all the more severely for denying him a pleasure he had
been counting on.

In the October, 1794, *Gentleman's Magazine* (962), Percy wrote the obituary of his cousin William Cleiveland with whom he had corresponded for about forty years.[17] He also wrote the obituary of his nephew Thomas Percy in the May, 1808, *Gentleman's Magazine* (470). Once a child prodigy like Thomas Romney Robinson, Percy's nephew published *Verses on the Death of Dr. Samuel Johnson* when he was fifteen, and he became a fellow of St. John's College, Oxford, and the rector of one of Percy's churches in the diocese of Dromore, where he seems to have been quite unhappy.[18] As we have seen, he was the nominal editor of the fourth edition of the *Reliques*; and, for a time, he was also Percy's choice as editor of the much talked about fourth volume. The obituary, understandably, does not reflect the growing distance between Percy and his nephew as the young man matured: "poor Tom never thinks about the Main Chance," Percy wrote to his wife on March 16, 1799, with the disappointment of one who generally does.[19]

The July, 1803, *European Magazine* (9–11) published a Percy article on Richard Rolt, a sequel to an exchange of letters between Rolt and Voltaire which, as Percy noted, "rescue the memory of Rolt from the injurious account with which it is degraded in the Biographia Dramatica . . . and by Boswell, in his Life of Johnson." Rolt, who had died in 1770, was survived for many years by his second wife, Percy's cousin Elizabeth Perrins, whom Percy (as he acknowledged in the anonymous article) "allowed a pension to her death."[20] The interest of the article centers in its account of the fortunes and misfortunes of "a professor of book-making and of the expedients to which want and need compelled him." These included the 1766 publication of Northall's *Travels through Italy*, which Rolt, though he had never been to Italy, compiled from the pocket diary of the deceased Captain John Northall "with the help of former printed travels." The article concludes with a "Catalogue" of twenty-two Rolt works, many of them "published without his name, and in weekly numbers."

II *Percy, Johnson, and the Johnson Circle*

Much of Percy's literary activity during the years following the publication of the *Reliques* was bound up with Johnson and members of the Johnson circle. As was noted earlier, Percy was introduced to Johnson by James Grainger in 1756, and the Percy-Johnson friendship was cultivated through Percy's numerous trips to London and Johnson's extended visit with the Percys at Easton Mauduit in the summer of 1764. In that year Percy and Johnson collaborated in a review of Grainger's poem *The Sugar Cane*,[21] though it is doubtful that Percy contributed much to the review, in spite of Johnson's statement to Boswell that "he only helped Percy with it, and was in jest."[22] Perhaps Johnson had in mind the extracts from the poem, which comprise the bulk of the review and may have been selected by Percy. A manuscript of the opening critical paragraphs in Johnson's handwriting leaves little room to question that he was their author;[23] and the fact that they are rather more uniformly laudatory of the poem than another review that he wrote of *The Sugar Cane*[24] suggests that Johnson may indeed have entered into the 1764 collaboration in jest. At the very least he must have had some difficulty taking a poem seriously which, in one of its drafts familiar to Johnson, had set off on a poetic flight with "Now, Muse, let's sing of *rats*."[25]

Grainger died young, like another early literary friend, William Shenstone, and Percy took a number of opportunities in his later years to rescue what he could of Grainger's reputation. His 1774 defense of Mrs. Grainger's character against a charge of flagrant infidelity to her husband was equally a defense of Grainger's memory.[26] In 1791 he persuaded Boswell to soften some Johnson remarks unflattering to Grainger which Boswell was about to publish in the *Life of Johnson*;[27] and seven years later, having commended Robert Anderson for his "article of my beloved friend Dr. Grainger" in Anderson's collection of the poets of Great Britain, he offered Anderson some unpublished Grainger poems for a future edition, and proceeded himself to write a brief account of Grainger for the *European Magazine*'s September, 1798, issue.[28] As for Shenstone, Percy seems to have written a substantial portion of the account of Shenstone's estate the Leasowes in the 1764 edition of Shenstone's works, but his precise contributions to the account remain undetermined.[29] He also edited the manuscript of *Shenstone's Miscellany*, though apparently with no intention of publication, and it remained in manuscript until 1952.[30]

If Johnson did not always share Percy's literary tastes—his opinion of Shenstone's poetry as well as of Grainger's was less favorable than Percy's—his and Goldsmith's friendship with Percy and their respect for his learning and ability doubtless opened the way for Percy's admission to the Club in 1768. In that year the withdrawal of John Hawkins and the Club's decision to expand its membership from ten to twelve created its first vacancies since its founding in 1764; and admitted along with Percy on February 15 were the dramatist George Colman and Robert Chambers, Vinerian Professor of Law at Oxford. Percy enjoyed and took pride in his membership, attended meetings when he was in London, and avidly sought news of the Club when he corresponded with Edmond Malone during his Dromore years. The Club was not such a fellowship, of course, that it resolved the differences of taste between Johnson and Percy or prompted Johnson to repress his disagreements with his younger clubmate. Johnson's well-known parody of *The Hermit of Warkworth,* for example, was delivered impromptu at a 1771 Oxford gathering when Johnson could no longer endure the praise of some persons present for the "Classical Simplicity" of Percy's poem:

> I put my hat upon my head
> And walked into the Strand,
> And there I met another man
> Whose hat was in his hand.

Johnson, savoring the triumph of the moment, declared that he could speak such poetry "extempore" for seven years together if he could find listeners dull enough to hear him.[31]

A less familiar Johnson parody was also uttered impromptu at Percy's expense, although privately to Mrs. Thrale rather than at a public gathering. Percy's translation of the Spanish poem "Rio Verde, Rio Verde," which he had printed at the end of the *Reliques*'s first volume, opened with the following stanza:

> Gentle river, gentle river,
>   Lo, thy streams are stain'd with gore,
> Many a brave and noble captain
>   Floats along thy willow'd shore.   (I, 319)

Mrs. Piozzi recorded in her *Anecdotes* that, when she commended the translation to Johnson, he replied that "he could do it better himself—as thus":

> Glassy water, glassy water,
> Down whose current clear and strong,
> Chiefs confus'd in mutual slaughter,
> Moor and Christian roll along.[32]

If the parody came to Percy's attention some years before its publication in the *Anecdotes*, it may help to account for his failure to publish *Ancient Songs Chiefly on Moorish Subjects* even after copperplates had been secured and the title page, dated 1775, had been set.[33] He was too astute a person to have missed the point of Johnson's *Hermit of Warkworth* parody, and too proud to invite further ridicule, as his Spanish translations would surely have done:

> Thro' Love's profound and stormy main
>   A hapless Mariner I sail,
> Nor hopes my weary bark to gain
>   Or welcome port or friendly gale.
>
> Led by a star my course I steer;
>   Ah! too remotely shine its rays;
> A lovelier star did ne'er appear
>   To Pilot's fond admiring gaze.[34]

The seven poems of *Ancient Songs* were held back, in any event, and they seem to have been the last of Percy's poetic translations, just as *The Hermit of Warkworth* seems to have been the last of his published original poems. Yet, however inadequate they were as translations, they show Percy once again at the edge of discovery. He was as much a pioneer in this effort as he had been with his translations of Chinese poetry in *Hau Kiou Choaan* and of Icelandic poetry in *Five Pieces of Runic Poetry*, for no one else in England was translating Spanish poetry which led to publication before the *Reliques* in 1765 or the proposed *Ancient Songs* of 1775.[35]

Had Percy been a member of the Club from the beginning, he would presumably have been invited like other Club members to submit notes for Johnson's edition of Shakespeare, which was published in 1765. Even as it was, Johnson supplemented his own note on a passage in *Othello* with a corrective note by Percy, probably prepared while Johnson was revising the proofs of *Othello* during his visit to Easton Mauduit in 1764.[36] Percy's interest in Shakespeare is, of course, apparent in the *Reliques*, with its ballads that illustrate Shakespeare, its mad songs, and Percy's own "The Friar of Orders Gray," a curiosity pressed together from the numerous snatches of song in Shakespeare's plays. On March 2, 1769, Percy himself took the initiative in securing a minor role in another of the Shakespeare editions by writing to Thomas Warton to suggest an improved glossary for the revision of the 1744 Hanmer Shakespeare soon to be published at Oxford. If he could see the glossary in manuscript, Percy commented, he "would make some additions to it, from a sketch of the same kind in MS. in my possession."[37] The offer was accepted, and the glossary was revised to include both Percy's notes and a number written into Percy's manuscript by John Hawkins.[38] In 1771 Percy sent materials to George Steevens, who incorporated "the greater part" of them in the Johnson-Steevens edition published in 1773 and reissued in 1778.[39] Even such a minor contribution as Percy's handful of notes did not escape the attention of Joseph Ritson in his 1783 *Remarks, Critical and Illustrative on the Text and Notes of the Last Edition of Shakespeare*. The "learned Prelate," wrote Ritson about a Percy note to *Henry VI*, part 2, "follows Dogberry's advice, and lets his writing and reading appear *when there is no need* of such vanity"(120).

Percy's relationship with Johnson never achieved the intimacy which the early association of the two men seemed to promise, and on at least one occasion it was strained almost to the breaking point. A dramatic episode in Boswell's *Life* records the angry exchange between Johnson and Percy over Thomas Pennant's comments about Alnwick Castle in his *Tour in Scotland. MDCCLXIX*, with the dispute ending peacefully only when Percy saw the need to inform Johnson that he had not meant to be "uncivil." Eleven days later, after Percy voiced his concern to Boswell that a young clergyman present might carry an unfavorable report of the incident to Percy's patron, Boswell secured from Johnson his well-known letter to Boswell in praise of Percy: "Percy's attention to poetry has given grace and splendour to his studies of antiquity." Johnson's understanding was that Boswell wanted the letter to show to Earl Percy, and thus he was much disturbed when Boswell confessed that he had given a copy to Percy himself, and he insisted that Boswell retrieve it. This conclusion of the episode was particularly mortifying to Percy, not merely because he had visions of the letter delighting his children and grandchildren, but also because he had no way of determining Johnson's motive for demanding the letter's return. Boswell, who naively thought that he had done everyone a good turn, was unable to enlighten him.[40]

That some distance separated Johnson and Percy is suggested by Percy's apparent neglect in not paying Johnson a farewell visit before he left in 1783 to settle in Dromore.[41] Their differences were not so numerous or significant, however, that they seriously diminished Percy's admiration and affection for Johnson. Percy's relationships with Boswell were another matter. For the *Life of Johnson* Percy supplied a variety of information, particularly about Johnson's early years, which Boswell found very useful. But Percy did not appreciate Boswell's refusal to honor his request for anonymity in his contributions, nor was he pleased with Boswell's treatment of him elsewhere in the book, including the planned revelation that Johnson had written the dedication for the *Reliques*. Shown the proofs of some sections, he argued vehemently and with some success for the suppression of the passage about the *Reliques* and of other passages in which Johnson, unjustly in Percy's view, censured the characters of James Grainger and Richard Rolt. The result, nonetheless, was by no means totally satisfactory to Percy, and the friendship and correspondence of the two men apparently ceased with the publication of the *Life of Johnson* in 1791.[42]

Percy's relationships with Robert Anderson appear to have been untroubled, though of course the third edition of Anderson's *Life of Johnson*, to which Percy also contributed, was not published until four years after Percy's death, so that he never had an opportunity to question Anderson's use of his materials. Had he lived, he would probably have been well pleased. In drawing his account of Johnson largely from the biographies of

Boswell and Sir John Hawkins, Anderson retained almost nothing that could give offense. There was no depreciation of Grainger or Rolt, and no reference to the dispute with Johnson over Pennant's *Tour in Scotland*. Anderson's tastes, in fact, were quite similar to Percy's, and his warm attachment to Percy's memory is evident in the eulogy stretched out in a note across six pages of his volume (250–55). Percy's contributions, moreover, are among the new edition's chief adornments: an account of Anna Williams, for example (298–99), a note on Garrick's mimickry of Johnson (50), a statement on the reason for Johnson's dislike of Swift (81), a note on Johnson's reception at Stourbridge when a boy (20), and Percy's acknowledgment of Johnson's role in writing the dedication of the *Reliques* (309). Anderson's biography has a special interest because of the medical and psychological insights which his experience as a physician permitted him, but Percy's contributions also helped to set it apart from the numerous lesser works about Johnson that competed for the public's favor against the major efforts of Boswell and Sir John Hawkins.[43]

Percy's most substantial literary work of his Dromore years, aside from the revised fourth edition of the *Reliques*, was the life of Goldsmith that prefaced the four-volume edition of Goldsmith's *Miscellaneous Works* published in 1801.[44] The 118-page biography may be said to have begun on April 28, 1773, during an interview in which Goldsmith dictated to Percy many of the essential facts of his life. After Goldsmith's death in 1774, Percy turned the memorial of the interview over to Johnson, along with other materials related to Goldsmith's life; but the hoped-for Johnson biography of Goldsmith was never written, and after Johnson's death the materials were returned to Percy by Edmond Malone in 1785.[45] On June 1 of that year, Percy issued proposals from Dublin for a subscription edition of *The Poetical Works of Dr. Oliver Goldsmith* for the benefit of Goldsmith's "only surviving Brother," with a new life of Goldsmith from original letters but chiefly from an account "Dictated by himself to A Gentleman who is in possession of the Manuscript." The projected edition was to be in one large quarto volume "elegantly printed on a Fine Paper," and subscriptions at one guinea were to be received by the publisher L. White in Dublin. [46]

Further delays followed, but about 1790 the Reverend Thomas Campbell was engaged by Percy to write the life of Goldsmith under his supervision. Campbell died on June 20, 1795, however, with the manuscript still incomplete, and after first employing the Reverend Henry Boyd for that purpose, Percy undertook to rewrite the manuscript himself. In doing so, as Richard L. Harp has shown, he retained Campbell's form for the biography, but altered his language almost throughout.[47] He also entrusted publication to the London firm of Cadell and Davies, who brought out the four-volume edition only after lengthy negotiation with Percy and after engaging Samuel Rose, without Percy's knowledge, to oversee the final editing. By that time, with Maurice Goldsmith having died in 1793, the proceeds of the publication were used for the benefit of a younger Goldsmith brother, Charles, who had not been known to Percy in 1785.[48]

For Percy the work was a continued vexation. His negotiations with Cadell and Davies were protracted, irritating, and in the end unsatisfying, and during the long period from 1785 to 1801 Thomas Campbell died, anticipated publishers died or withdrew, and the changing situation of Goldsmith's relations kept him in constant uncertainty as to who in fact was to benefit from the publication. In addition to suffering the humiliation of being replaced as final editor by Samuel Rose, who intruded a number of anecdotes into the biography, he was denied a sight of the proof sheets and so harshly maligned by his publishers that he felt impelled to prepare a statement of "what passed between D[r] Percy . . . and Mess[rs] Cadell and Davies."[49]

For all the help that he solicited and did not solicit, the life of Goldsmith remains largely Percy's work, and its 118 pages constituted the first really substantial and authoritative biography. Samuel Glover's memoir, written immediately after Goldsmith's death, was a slender sketch, hardly more than a hasty memorial suited to one of the monthly magazines.[50] Percy, who seems to have been Goldsmith's choice as biographer, had the advantage of an eighteen-year association with Goldsmith and of a variety of original materials, some of which he had obtained from Goldsmith himself and some through subsequent inquiry. These included reminiscing letters from Goldsmith relations and ten letters of Goldsmith himself, a significant start in bringing together a correspondence which, in Katharine Balderston's edition, numbers only fifty-three letters known to have been written by Goldsmith.[51] Percy's procedure, like William Mason's in his life of Gray, was generally to insert the entire letters, so that his narrative at times provides little more than a connecting link between them.

Percy was both partial to his subject and sensitive to the demands of decorum, and he selected many of his details accordingly. He omitted, for example, much of the material about Goldsmith in Boswell's *Life of Johnson* in which he thought Goldsmith unfairly treated; and when a dubious trait of character was too familiar or too well established to be overlooked, he tried to see it in context:

He is . . . supposed to have been often soured by jealousy or envy; and many little instances are mentioned of this tendency in his character: but whatever appeared of this kind was a mere momentary sensation, which he knew not how like other men to conceal. It was never the result of principle, or the suggestion of reflection; it never imbittered his heart, nor influenced his conduct. Nothing could be more amiable than the general features of his mind: those of his person were not perhaps so engaging. (I, 117)

Thus, for all Percy's partiality, there was no canonization. Nor did he yield to the temptation romantically to equate Goldsmith with characters in his own works. *The Vicar of Wakefield* and *The Deserted Village,* source books of later biographers, were left almost unexamined. He was aware, of course, that Goldsmith merited attention as an eminent poet, novelist, playwright, essayist, biographer, and historian, but he was content by and large to let the works and their reputations speak for themselves.

The book as a result is primarily factual rather than interpretive or critical, and its preeminent contribution, as might have been expected of Percy, is that it rescued numerous important materials which might soon have been beyond recovery. If it does not sparkle it does at times glow with the warmth of Percy's recollections of one of his earliest literary friends:

The Doctor was writing his Enquiry, &c. in a wretched dirty room, in which there was but one chair, and when he, from civility, offered it to his visitant [Percy], himself was obliged to sit in the window. While they were conversing, some one gently rapped at the door, and being desired to come in, a poor ragged little girl of very decent behaviour, entered, who, dropping a curtsie, said, "My mamma sends her compliments, and begs the favour of you to lend her a chamber-pot full of coals. (I, 61)

Although Goldsmith was never quite so intimate a Percy friend as Shenstone and Grainger, the book makes clear that he always retained his hold on Percy's admiration and affection, a power he has exerted on generations ever since.

CHAPTER 6

The Percy Correspondence and the
Influence of the Reliques

PERCY's mind was constantly active, and the need to find answers to his endless questions, to provide information, and to share a thought or extend a greeting drove him inexorably to his pen. He scribbled in books and notebooks, on old manuscripts, and on scraps of paper. Time and again he crammed the quarto and octavo sheets of his letters to capacity, with postscripts squeezed in at the end, at the top of the first page, and vertically in the margins. His earliest letter to survive was written in 1750 to a fellow Oxford student. His last was written to his daughter Barbara on August 28, 1811, about a month before his death. Some 2,500 letters to and from him have made their way into private collections and public archives, and about half of them have been printed.[1] Among eighteenth-century literary figures, few persons exceed him in the sheer volume of his published letters.

I *The Correspondence*

The bulk of Percy's published correspondence is contained in two collections separated by about a century. *Illustrations of the Literary History of the Eighteenth Century,* begun by John Nichols in 1818 and completed by his son in 1858, devotes a good part of its final three volumes to Percy's correspondences with James Grainger, George Steevens, Robert Anderson, and others. *The Percy Letters,* initiated by David Nichol Smith and Cleanth Brooks in 1944 with the correspondence of Percy and Edmond Malone, continued with Percy's correspondences with Richard Farmer, Thomas Warton, Lord Hailes, Evan Evans,

George Paton and (after a pause of sixteen years) William Shenstone.[2] Other letters have appeared in articles and books, including collections of the correspondence of such writers as David
Hume, Oliver Goldsmith, James Boswell, and Samuel Johnson.

This array of names suggests the range and significance of
Percy's correspondence. Percy was in touch with many of the
intellectual leaders of his day—Walpole, Garrick, Reynolds, and
(at the end of Percy's life) Walter Scott may be added to those
already mentioned—and he almost always managed to find a
common ground with his correspondents, for the exchange of
views, if not for agreement. Even so unlikely a person as David
Hume is said to have been a Percy guest at the chaplain's table
in St. James's Palace,[3] and in a correspondence stretched out
for a year Percy attempted to persuade Hume that the fifteenth-
century earl of the *Northumberland Houshold Book* was not
given to a "niggardly" management of his household, as Hume
had asserted in the 1773 edition of his *History of England*.[4]

Like the correspondence with Hume, many of Percy's correspondences were brief, but a number were sustained for one or
more decades, some of them with intermittent gaps of a year
or more. Two of those in which Percy took the most obvious
pleasure were cut short by the untimely deaths of William Shenstone in 1763 and James Grainger in 1766, but even from the
little more than five years of the Percy-Shenstone friendship
about fifty letters have survived, and some forty letters attest
to the warmth of the Grainger-Percy attachment over a ten-year
period.[5] The fates dealt more kindly with other Percy friends.
The correspondence with Thomas Warton was nurtured, even
if it did not always flourish, for seventeen years, the Percy-Farmer
correspondence for sixteen years, and the Percy-Hailes for
twenty-seven. The longest of Percy's scholarly correspondences,
with Edmond Malone, was begun in 1779 and continued until
1811, the year of Percy's death, and, like that with Robert Anderson from 1798 to 1811, it brought Percy a much needed solace
and cheer during his declining years in far-off Dromore.

Letters in print span the fifty-five year period from 1756 to
1811, and not a single year of that period is unrepresented. The
longest gap is for the five months between October, 1793, and
March, 1794. Understandably the years of greatest abundance,

at least of Percy's own letters, are those from 1761 to 1765, when his ingenious network of scholarly friends in England, Scotland, and Wales was helping him to ready the *Reliques* for its 1765 publication. These years stand out in part because latter-day scholars have taken a natural interest in the background of the *Reliques* which they vividly reflect; but they were the years of his most frequent correspondence in any event, at least until the end of the century. At that time the Irish rebellion of 1798 compelled him to settle his family in England while he remained in Dublin or Dromore, where he filled his letters to his wife with news of the insurrection, the Irish Parliament, and the Percy household and garden at Dromore.[6] Only after the vote for the union of England and Ireland in 1800 did he feel free to join her in England for a brief sojourn.

In their concentration upon his scholarly work, Percy's letters, particularly of the 1760s and 1770s, have provided fascinating insights both into the *Reliques of Ancient English Poetry* and into the workings of an unusually perceptive, disciplined, and well furnished mind. Percy had clear objectives when he entered on a scholarly quest, and he normally drove straight to the mark. "Since I left you," he wrote to Thomas Warton on March 3, 1769,

I have been reflecting on the New Edition of Hanmer's Shakespeare which deficient and inferior, as it will be, in many respects, to what one would wish it; may yet have one advantage beyond any of the former Editions: And that is in having a good *Glossary* to it. . . . [If] I could see . . . [a Copy of the Glossary] in Manuscript I would make some additions to it, from a sketch of the same kind in MS. in my own possession.[7]

His command of detail is astonishing. Names, dates, subjects, titles, allusions, quotations poured from his pen, not in disorderly profusion but with a precision that constantly excites admiration. He inspired such confidence in his ability and integrity that Richard Farmer not only borrowed some of Cambridge University's rare books for his use but actually sent the books to him at Easton Mauduit; and the Advocates Library in Edinburgh permitted him to retain the priceless and irreplaceable Bannatyne Manuscript of old poems in his possession for over two years.

The volumes of *The Percy Letters*, with their concentration upon seven correspondences, afford a variety of glimpses into Percy's character. With Farmer he is friendly and jocular, much at his ease—a reflection of their personal and scholarly compatibility. With Evans he is the aggressive scholar pressing for information about a literature and a culture of which he barely knows the rudiments. With Shenstone he is the younger friend and aspiring editor drawing upon the judgment and taste of an admired and experienced poet. With Malone he is the congenial clubmate, an elder scholar sharing his thoughts with a fellow scholar, a distant friend clinging to the country and society of his happiest years and never surfeited with news of them. In focusing attention on his scholarly correspondence, however, *The Percy Letters* has sometimes left the impression of a man so hedged about with scholarship that the human being is not readily visible: "one never feels that one has seen into his deeper nature," wrote Bertrand Bronson.[8] Bronson's "never" is too strong a word, but Percy's deeper nature might have been better displayed if attention had also been directed to some of his more intimate correspondences: with the friend of his bachelor years in Easton Mauduit, Thomas Apperley, for example; with William Cleiveland, the revered cousin with whom he corresponded on personal family and clerical matters for close to forty years; or with his wife. "In the little walled park fronting my Dining Room window," he writes from Dromore on June 15, 1799, to Mrs. Percy at Tunbridge Wells,

I am much amused by my Tonquin sow & Litter of little Pigs, who are running among the Trees, and now know me so well, as I frequently throw them the young shoots of Trees, that whenever I look over the wall they come running to me. . . . they have a very singular Companion—a large Chicken . . . [born in the great Snow, left by its Mother, and] nursed in the house by my Servants: when it was turned abroad it found the warmth of the Straw in the Hogstye so much more comfortable than the Hen-Roost that it has ever associated with the Pigs, & is for ever attending these little Things in the day time, & at night always roosts on a Pig's back, where it often sits in the day time. . . . As for the little play things, they are now fit for the Spit, but I can not bring myself to kill them.[9]

Nonetheless, the emphasis in *The Percy Letters* upon Percy's scholarly activities, particularly as they related to the *Reliques,* can hardly be considered misplaced. The *Reliques* was Percy's great work, and the primary if not the sole reason that he is remembered today. Interest in Percy's correspondence itself began with the *Reliques* and has been sustained by it ever since. It has been useful, moreover, to be reminded—perhaps even to see for the first time—that Percy was one of the most industrious, learned, and imaginative scholars in an age of unprecedented scholarly achievement, and that those qualities were best exemplified in the *Reliques.* For nineteenth-century editors, taking up the Ritson cudgels, battered Percy's reputation almost beyond restoration, until scholars like Albert Friedman and the editors of *The Percy Letters* supplied the means to see his work minutely and in context.

Percy may be said to have benefited from extraordinary good luck in his scholarly endeavors, but a man of his imagination and industry inevitably created much of his own good luck. The pioneering spirit that led him to edit the *Northumberland Household Book,* to publish a Chinese novel, to translate Icelandic and Spanish poetry—to seek out the early poetry of various nations—also led him to discover materials that were suited to his needs. The Chinese manuscripts were made available to him because he perceived their interest and value and inspired enough confidence to have the owner grant his request to borrow them. Cleanth Brooks, in discussing Percy's work on the abortive edition of Surrey's poems, notes that the only three extant copies of one of the earliest settings of *Tottel's Miscellany* (1557) have a Percy connection, "proved or conjectured";[10] and obviously they came into Percy's hands, not by coincidence, but because he was diligent and thorough in his inquiries. His discovery of the folio manuscript was of course the most dramatic, the rescuing of priceless treasures from imminent destruction. It was indeed a stroke of good fortune that Percy happened upon the manuscript before Humphrey Pitt's servants had gone any further with its incineration, but it was characteristic of Percy that he had the presence of mind to look into the manuscript, to ask for it, and to preserve it until further study permitted him to appreciate its interest and to share it with the public.

By that time Percy was a poet, an editor, and a pioneering scholar given at times to imitating the styles of other poets and to adapting ancient works for modern readers. He was also the friend of other poets and scholars, most particularly of William Shenstone, whose advice he looked to even if he was not always prepared to be led by it. The volumes of *The Percy Letters* lift the curtain on an editorial drama of unusual excitement and complexity—of discovery and disappointment, imagination and obtuseness, grand schemes and minutiae, principle and compromise, delight and sorrow. Part of the drama involved also a process of mending and patching that Percy, poet and editor that he was, applied to some of his manuscript fragments in the hope either of restoring them to something like their original states or of making them otherwise acceptable to the public.

It was, of course, this aspect of Percy's editorial practice that sent tremors of rage through nineteenth-century editorial circles, epitomized in Frederick J. Furnivall and John W. Hales, the editors of the 1867–1868 *Bishop Percy's Folio Manuscript*. Percy looked on the text of the folio manuscript, wrote Furnivall, "as a young woman from the country with unkempt locks, whom he had to fit for fashionable society. . . . He puffed out the 39 lines of the *Child of Ell* to 200; he pomatumed the *Heir of Lin* till it shone again; he stuffed bits of wool into *Sir Cawline, Sir Aldingar*; he powdered everything" (I, xvi–xvii). The indictment was graphic and comprehensive, and it is understandable that subsequent scholars were to find it difficult to forgive or to defend Percy's handiwork.

II *The Influence of the* Reliques

The negative impact of the *Reliques*, most conspicuous in the reactions, first of Joseph Ritson and later of Furnivall and Hales, had of course its positive aspect also, since it stimulated numerous scholars to search out correct or supplementary texts or otherwise to try to undo the harm they considered Percy to have done. Such an influence, it goes without saying, cannot be cited to Percy's advantage. And when one attempts to assess his clearly

positive influences one confronts the obvious facts that Percy
was neither the first nor the last of his century's ballad collectors
and thus may have to share any credit with numerous others,
and that influences upon individuals and cultures are often so
varied and complex as to defy precise allocation. These are
useful cautions against claiming too much for a favorite. Yet the
evidence both of Percy's own time and of subsequent decades
leads unmistakeably to the conclusion that, of all such compilations, the *Reliques* had by far the most profound and pervasive
influence.

A century that began by relishing a 1685 Latin translation of
"Chevy Chase" needed considerable conditioning to make it
ready for the rough-hewn verses that were the staple of Percy's
folio manuscript. If Joseph Addison's *Spectator* essays of 1710
signaled the end of Latinized ballads, their influence was hardly
sufficient to assure the ancient ballads a currency in eighteenth-
century literary circles. Even by 1765, when the *Reliques* was
published, the leading periodical of the day could review Percy's
efforts with a high degree of skepticism and condescension.
This collection, wrote the *Gentleman's Magazine,*

will please persons that have a taste for genuine poetry, chiefly
as an object of curiosity; here and there however will be found some
approaches to harmony, and here and there some poetical beauties
of a superior kind. There is a class of readers and of writers too, that
profess themselves to be admirers of *simplicity,* to delight in the
stanza of *Spencer,* and to prefer both our language and our versification in their rudiments to the correct elegance of later times. To these
gentlemen this work will afford great pleasure, setting curiosity
wholly aside. (vol. 35, pt. 1, p. 180)

To the 1765 *Gentleman's Magazine,* in other words, the ballads
of Percy's collection fell somewhat short of "genuine poetry."
Essentially they constituted a curiosity, not without superior
"beauties," to be sure, but clearly wanting the "correct elegance"
of modern times. Yet in less than thirty years the same magazine
could undertake an appreciative series on the *Reliques* and
sustain it through eleven issues spanning the more than two
years between August, 1793, and September, 1795.[11]

The years between were marked by a steady evolution in English taste almost beyond question given its major impetus by Percy's *Reliques*. By 1793 three editions of the *Reliques* had been published and the *Gentleman's Magazine* series was written (by someone unknown to Percy, the writer said) in anticipation of the fourth. The *Reliques* had been followed by David Herd's *Ancient and Modern Scots Songs* in 1769; Thomas Evans's *Old Ballads, Historical and Narrative* in 1777; John Pinkerton's *Scottish Tragic Ballads* in 1781 and *Select Scottish Ballads* in 1783, the year of Joseph Ritson's *Select Collection of English Songs*; an expansion of Evans's *Old Ballads* from two to four volumes in 1784; Charlotte Brooke's *Reliques of Ancient Irish Poetry* in 1789; and Ritson's *Ancient Songs* in 1790 and *Pieces of Ancient Popular Poetry* in 1791. Gates left ajar by earlier editors, in short, had been flung open wide by Percy in 1765, and however much his successors may have supplemented or amended his contributions, he remained for his and for subsequent generations the very symbol of the revival of interest in the ballads. That even the title of the *Reliques* was thought to possess a special magic is witnessed by Charlotte Brooke's adaptation of it for her volume of Irish poetry and a similar adaptation by Robert Jamieson for his 1806 *Popular Ballads and Songs*, which he subtitled *Reliques of Ancient Scottish Poetry*.

The second edition of Thomas Evans's *Old Ballads* further underscores the extent to which the *Reliques* had become the measure of the new ballad interest. Turning his own half title into a puff, Evans notes that his volumes contain poems ancient, modern, and original, "None of which are inserted in Dr. Percy's Collection." For information on the minstrels, he concludes his preface by referring his readers to Percy's "very ingenious essay" in the *Reliques*. And in the "Advertisement" he quotes with satisfaction a comment in the *Critical Review* of April, 1777, concerning the first edition of *Old Ballads*: "The success of Dr. Percy's collection of old ballads has instigated Mr. Evans to furnish that supplement to it which is at present under our consideration" (XLII, 313). Evans, it might be added, astutely followed Percy into his own household to secure a well-placed patron for his collection: *Old Ballads* is dedicated to the duke of Northumberland.

Looking back fondly to old times and old ways had become increasingly fashionable since the publication of Macpherson's Ossian poems and poems like Gray's "The Bard." Perhaps an age that could draw inspiration from the graveyard was destined more and more to glorify the graveyard's inhabitants. Robin Hood grew from one poem in the *Reliques* to twenty-seven in *Old Ballads* and thirty-three in Ritson's *Robin Hood* of 1795. Antiquarian scholarship, of course, had developed strong roots in Britain, and as early as 1717 the Society of Antiquaries, after some years of informal gatherings, had been formally reconstituted in London. But antiquarians tended then as now to speak only to other antiquarians, and the ridicule heaped upon the pedant by men like Jonathan Swift and Alexander Pope had its milder counterpart later in the century in Johnson's dismissal of the mere antiquarian as "a rugged being." *Archaeologia* and *The Antiquarian Repertory* confirm Johnson's characterization on page after page, not excluding some of those occupied by Percy's contributions. The antiquarians were plainly incapable of stimulating a general revival of interest in the past.

But Percy was more talented and flexible than most of his contemporaries, and, antiquarian though he was, he was able to reach the wider public that he and Shenstone had contemplated in their discussions of editorial practice. Throughout the *Reliques* the poet in him broke through the rugged barriers of his antiquarianism, and no one responded more enthusiastically than the poets themselves. E. H. W. Meyerstein, the biographer of Thomas Chatterton, thought that the *Reliques* "might almost be called the efficient poetical cause of Rowley" and saw in "Brystowe Tragedy" an attempt by Chatterton to produce a ballad that would compare favorably with those in the *Reliques*.[12] James Beattie acknowledged that the "hint" of his popular *The Minstrel* was taken from the "Essay on the Ancient English Minstrels."[13] Margaret Lowery in *Windows of the Morning* charted William Blake's indebtedness to the *Reliques*, and G. E. Bentley noted that Blake's "Mad Song" is a composite of the six mad songs in Percy's second volume.[14]

Percy comes into his own, however, with the Romantic poets of the early nineteenth century. His brief correspondence with Walter Scott, encouraged by their mutual friend Dr. Robert

Anderson, seems almost a linking of the two centuries, a symbolic passing on of the mantle of ballad editorship from the aging Percy to the young Scott, whose forthcoming *Minstrelsy of the Scottish Border* was deeply indebted to the *Reliques*. On January 11, 1801, Scott acknowledged receipt of his first letter from Percy by confessing that he felt as he did "when the Reliques of Ancient Poetry were first put into my hands, an era in my poetical taste which I shall never forget." "The very grass sod seat," Scott continued, "to which (when a boy of twelve years old) I retreated from my playfellows, to devour the works of the ancient minstrels, is still fresh and dear to my memory."[15] Wordsworth and Coleridge left no romantic record of their introduction to the *Reliques*, but it seems evident that its three volumes came to them as a revelation also. In a memorable tribute, Wordsworth contrasted the effect of Ossian with that of the *Reliques*, which he found

so unassuming, so modest in . . . [its] pretensions!—I have already stated how much Germany is indebted to this latter work; and for our own country, its poetry has been absolutely redeemed by it. I do not think that there is an able writer in verse of the present day who would not be proud to acknowledge his obligations to the "Reliques;" I know that it is so with my friends; and, for myself, I am happy in this occasion to make a public avowal of my own.[16]

Probably the very title of the *Lyrical Ballads* was owing to the *Reliques*, with which ballads were all but synonymous by the end of the century, and in the *Reliques* the two poets found those qualities that appealed to their very different temperaments and talents. The ballad stanza proved attractive to both, as it did to many of Percy's successors. But Wordsworth was drawn most to those ballads that portrayed common people and the simple life in language free of the eighteenth-century poetic diction that he disliked, whereas Coleridge derived his stimulus rather from the supernatural in Percy's ballads, and was affected more by their archaisms than by what Wordsworth thought of as the language of men. "The Children in the Wood" in Percy's collection was a Wordsworth favorite, a stanza of which he quoted in his preface to the second edition of *Lyrical Ballads* as an example of a worthy subject expressed in appropriate conversational English, As John L. Mahoney noted, the poem is further reflected in the opening lines of Wordsworth's poem "The Redbreast."[17] Coleridge introduced "Dejection: an Ode" with the vivid stanza from "Sir Patrick Spence" in which the Scottish sailor reports ominously that "late yestreen" he saw the old moon with the new moon in her arm. In "The Rime of the Ancient Mariner" John Livingston Lowes detected echoes of theme from "The Wandering Jew" and of language from "Chevy Chase," "The Battle of Otterbourne," "Edom O' Gordon," and "Sir Cauline."[18]

For Wordsworth, unlike Coleridge, the lyrical quality of the lyrical ballad was generally more important than the narrative implicit in the word "ballad." His "The White Doe of Rylstone," a poem in seven cantos built upon the story of "The Rising in the North," typically subordinates the narrative of the *Reliques*'s 152-line ballad to what Stephen Maxfield Parrish calls "the internal movements of imagination and feeling in the minds and hearts of the characters."[19] "Lady Bothwell's Lament" is adapted more sparely in Wordsworth's "The Mad Mother," but nonetheless at twice the length of Percy's original. In Percy's poem a deserted mother still in love with her betrayer sings to her sleeping child and bids him never to become like his father. Wordsworth's is a mad song—perhaps indebted to that group in the *Reliques* also—of a deserted mother who has stopped beneath a haystack in the woods to suckle her child and to sing to it, disjointedly, of her fancies, including returning to her husband. The six-line stanzas in octosyllabic couplets of the original are expanded to ten lines rhyming a a b b c d c d e e, and a refrain is abandoned. What the *Reliques* supplied was a compellingly written model, essentially a song on the traditional theme of the false lover, with the mother's love for the child and bitterness against her betrayer unfolded with exemplary restraint:

> Farewell, farewell, thou falsest youth,
> That evir kist a womans mouth!
> I wish all maides be warnd by mee
> Nevir to trust mans curtesy;
> For if we doe bot chance to bow,

> They'le use us than they care nae how.
> Balow, my babe, ly stil, and sleipe,
> It greives me sair to see thee weipe.   (II, 196)

Wordsworth shapes the poem into a study of a deranged mind, and exploits not just the pathos of the mother's situation but also the dramatic contrast between her motherly and wifely resolves and the ravings that betray her incompetence:

> . . . I will always be thy guide,
> Through hollow snows and rivers wide
> I'll build an Indian bower; I know
> The leaves that make the softest bed:
> And if from me thou wilt not go,
> But still be true 'till I am dead,
> My pretty thing! then thou shalt sing,
> As merry as the birds in spring.[20]

It is a less formal, more personal song, although it is no more moving than "Lady Bothwell's Lament." What is interesting to see, however, is how Wordsworth, who characteristically had an actual person in mind, could adapt an ancient poem on a traditional theme to his own purposes and to a poetic style that was highly untraditional.

Many of the poems in the *Reliques* were equally adaptable to Wordsworth's purposes or those of other poets and one might go on citing poems in which the influence of the *Reliques* is apparent—Wordsworth's Yarrow poems, for example, indebted by Wordsworth's own acknowledgment to William Hamilton's "The Braes of Yarrow" in volume 2 of the *Reliques*. Indeed, it is a tribute both to Percy's choice of poems for restoration and to the quality of his work that the poems in the *Reliques* from which Wordsworth and Coleridge drew their greatest inspiration included two or three with those alterations that Furnivall was to find most offensive. Somehow the two poets never noticed the powder and the bits of wool. Wordsworth thought "Sir Cauline" "exquisite"; and that poem, "The Child of Elle," and "The Marriage of Sir Gawaine"—only half a poem in the folio manuscript—have all been shown to have influenced Coleridge's

"Christabel," in which even the heroine's name was derived from Percy's addition to "Sir Cauline."[21]

We today, aware of Percy's transforming hand, can hardly read these poems in the spirit of his late eighteenth- and early nineteenth-century admirers. He far exceeded the limits that Shenstone had suggested and left no adequate index to his handiwork. Yet he almost certainly preserved a number of poems from oblivion, for Percy could hardly have expected to arouse public interest in ballads mutilated virtually beyond recognition. Nor is it an exaggeration to say that, as much as any of the *Reliques*'s treasures, they drew the attention of Percy's contemporaries and the Romantic poets to the wonders of ballad literature. As early as 1765 the *Critical Review* praised "The Child of Elle" as "a most beautiful ballad," which the reviewer did not perceive to have been "puffed out" by Percy from thirty-nine lines to two hundred.[22] Percy's changes, of course, were not confined to the comparatively few poems given major revision. Almost nothing escaped his editorial pencil as he strove to make the poems acceptable to his late eighteenth-century readers. In the end, as we have seen, he justified his practice on the success of his efforts.

He was right to do so, and by and large it was a sufficient justification. The interest and, ultimately, the ferment that Percy induced are indisputable, and no one can give assurance that if in 1765 he had published his ballads as he found them they would have had anything like the impact they are known to have had. Even in 1802 Scott was not willing to run such a risk with his *Minstrelsy of the Scottish Border.* He edited his poems much in the manner of Percy.

The influence of the *Reliques,* it must be emphasized, goes far beyond that of individual poems. Wordsworth's comment about its effect upon Germany was amply documented in 1904 by Elsie I. M. Boyd,[23] who noted that a translation of eleven of the *Reliques*'s poems was published at Göttingen as early as 1767. But the first English edition was itself widely circulated in Germany, and Boyd found an "astounding change" in the work of Bürger as a result of his reading the *Reliques* in 1770, about the same time that Herder was inspired by the *Reliques* to undertake his own collection of folksongs. Herder's *Volkslieder,* published in 1778 and 1779, contained twenty-seven ballads traceable to the *Reliques*. Other translations of poems in the *Reliques* followed, and German poets went to Percy either directly in his English edition or indirectly through his translators and Herder's compilation. Goethe's last ballad was derived from both "The Beggar's Daughter of Bednall-Green" and "King Cophetua and the Beggar-Maid"; and altogether Boyd found ninety-one poems in the *Reliques* which existed in one or more later German versions.

In Britain, as in Germany, the profoundest effect of the *Reliques* was in the spirit with which it suffused the age that followed it. The new currency given the ballad and the ballad stanza, the new delight in England's medieval heritage, the release afforded the imagination by a literature and a mythology only dimly perceived until Percy brought them into the light—these were the inexhaustible legacy of the *Reliques*. The sheer variety of Percy's 175 poems gave them a stature that no other collection achieved. They are a commonwealth of court, city, and hamlet, of palace and cottage, of king and shepherd, knight and knave, earl and artisan, fair maid and loathly lady, heroes real and legendary—St. George, King Arthur, Sir Gawaine and Sir Lancelot, Robin Hood, Hotspur and Douglas, the very figure of the minstrel himself. They are filled with surprises and strange turnings of the way. Poems illuminate each other. Burlesque yields to exultant celebration, "The Turnament of Tottenham" to "For the Victory at Agincourt" (II, 13–25). "Lord Thomas and Fair Ellinor," a love-tragedy born of a mother's cruel use of power, takes Percy immediately to John Lily's "Cupid and Campaspe," in which a lover finds reason to wonder how his mistress will use her power upon him (III, 82–86). Sir John Suckling in "Why So Pale?" supplies the wisdom we have just seen wanting in the hapless swain of "The Baffled Knight," ducked in the castle moat in his fourth attempt upon a maiden's virtue: "If of herself she will not love,/ Nothing can make her./ The devil take her!" (III, 238–46). Here in the *Reliques*'s extraordinary range of experience—of subject, theme, character, mood, and story—was provision for a century of imaginative poets, for a Keats, a Tennyson, and a Rossetti as well as for a Blake, a Wordsworth, and a Coleridge.

Here also was the justification of the countless hours Percy had spent with Shenstone poring through the old collections of poems, rating, selecting, and arranging; of the week and a half at Cambridge tediously transcribing from the broadside ballads amassed by Samuel Pepys; of the long and frequent letters to Shenstone, Farmer, Warton, Evans, and Lord Hailes; of his alertness in preserving the folio manuscript from destruction in the home of Humphrey Pitt. It is not surprising that the four editions of the *Reliques* in Percy's lifetime[24] were succeeded by ten to fifteen times that number, beginning with the fifth edition in the year after his death and continuing into our own time; nor can we be surprised, when we recall Sir Walter Scott's boyhood enchantment with the *Reliques,* that *The Boy's Percy* was published and went through numerous editions between 1882 and 1923. Generation after generation was introduced to English poetry by Thomas Percy.

Ballad publication reached its height in the nineteenth century, first with William Motherwell's 1827 *Minstrelsy Ancient and Modern,* and most notably with Francis J. Child's comprehensive collection of ballads and ballad variants published between 1882 and 1898 as *The English and Scottish Popular Ballads.* But the elaborate and discriminating scholarship of that period drew its first breath from the work of Percy, who approached his study of the ballads with more seriousness than he ever admitted to, and with more perception than has at times been acknowledged. In its simplest terms, his contribution was England's greatest anthology. In Wordsworth's, it was the absolute redemption of English poetry.

Notes and References

Chapter One

1. *Illustrations of the Literary History of the Eighteenth Century*, ed. John Nichols and John Bowyer Nichols (London, 1817–1858), VII, 116; hereafter cited as *Lit. Illus.*

2. *Reliques of Ancient English Poetry* (London, 1765), I, xiv.

3. *The Percy Letters*, vol. 4; *The Correspondence of Thomas Percy & David Dalrymple, Lord Hailes*, ed. A. F. Falconer (Baton Rouge: Louisiana State University Press, 1954), p. 30.

4. The baptismal entry in the register of St. Leonard, Bridgnorth uses the spelling *Pearcy*, but Percy commonly signed his letters *Thomas Piercy* until the summer of 1756.

5. British Library Add. Ms. 32,326, f. 21. The manuscript contains Percy's account of his own life. A very useful published article based largely on the manuscript is J. F. A. Mason, "Bishop Percy's Account of His Own Education," *Notes and Queries*, 204 (November, 1959), 404–8.

6. British Library Add. Ms. 32,326, f. 25.

7. The information comes from the parish registers of St. Calixtus, Astley Abbots and St. Peter and St. Paul, Tasley. Both registers are kept at St. Leonard, Bridgnorth.

8. Information from the parish registers of St. Peter and St. Paul, Easton Mauduit and St. Mary the Virgin, Wilby. I have used the eighteenth-century spelling (Easton *Mauduit* rather than *Maudit*) throughout the text and notes.

9. Parish register, Easton Mauduit.

10. British Library Add. Ms. 32,333, f. 16.

11. *The Miscellaneous Works of Oliver Goldsmith, M.D.* (London, 1801), I, 62–63.

12. British Library Add. Ms. 32,335, f. 155.

13. For an account of this period of Percy's life, see Cleanth Brooks, "The Country Parson as Research Scholar: Thomas Percy, 1760–1770," *The Papers of the Bibliographical Society of America*, 53 (3d quarter, 1959), 219–39.

14. James Boswell, *The Life of Samuel Johnson, LL.D.*, ed. G. B.

Hill, revised by L. F. Powell (Oxford: Clarendon Press, 1934–1950), III, 273.

15. *Lit. Illus.*, VIII, 191–92.

16. British Library Add. Ms. 32,333, f. 159v.

17. Ibid., f. 161.

18. Letter Percy to William Maginis, Dec. 6, 1791, Bodleian Ms. Percy c. 1, ff. 151–52 (printed in *Wilby Parish Magazine*, no. 30 [June, 1901]); also letter Percy to Lord Primate of Ireland, March 16, 1798, ibid., ff. 175–76.

Chapter Two

1. Boswell, *Life of Johnson*, III, 278.

2. Alexander Pope, *Minor Poems*, ed. Norman Ault and John Butt (London: Methuen, 1954), p. 302.

3. *Shenstone's Miscellany 1759–1763*, ed. Ian A. Gordon (Oxford: Clarendon Press, 1952), p. 48. The author of the 1720 "Letter of Advice to a Young Poet" (long thought to be Jonathan Swift) noted at the end of the letter that the fool and the chaplain were often united in one person (Jonathan Swift, *Satires and Personal Writings*, ed. W. A. Eddy [London: Oxford University Press, 1933], p. 58).

4. *Shenstone's Miscellany*, pp. 53–54: 137–38.

5. British Library Add. Ms. 32,336, f. 9v (May 25, 1756).

6. Anna Williams, *Miscellanies in Prose and Verse* (London, 1766), p. 3. Percy's copy is in the library of Queen's University of Belfast.

7. *Universal Visiter*, May 1756, p. 240. The poem was reprinted in the *St. James's Magazine*, February, 1764, p. 363.

8. Ibid., July, 1756, pp. 330–31.

9. *Lit. Illus.*, VII, 247.

10. *Grand Magazine of Universal Intelligence*, February, 1758, p. 96; March, 1758, p. 145.

11. *A Collection of Poems by Several Hands*, ed. Robert Dodsley (London, 1758), VI, 233–39.

12. James Johnson, *The Scots Musical Museum* (Edinburgh, 1787), I, 33; William Stenhouse, *Illustrations of the Lyric Poetry and Music of Scotland* (Edinburgh, 1853), pp. 29–31.

13. *Gentleman's Magazine*, August, 1780, p. 372. Warton's authorship of the article, which is signed J. W., was first suggested by George Lyman Kittredge in "Percy and His Nancy," *The Manly Anniversary Studies in Language and Literature* (Chicago: University of Chicago Press, 1923), p. 211, n. 4.

14. John Aiken, *Essays in Song Writing*, 2d ed. (Warrington, 1774), p. 110.

15. *The Letters of Robert Burns*, ed. J. DeLancey Ferguson (Oxford: Clarendon Press, 1931), II, 126; Kittredge, "Percy and His Nancy," p. 211.

16. The English text is from Dodsley's *Collection of Poems*. The Scottish variants are from Kittredge's "Percy and His Nancy," for which Kittredge made use of a Percy manuscript of the poem at Harvard (bMS Eng 893 [257]). My use of the manuscript has been by permission of the Houghton Library.

17. *The Works of Allan Ramsay*, ed. Alexander M. Kinghorn and Alexander Law (Edinburgh: William Blackwood, 1961), III, 67.

18. National Library of Scotland, Ms. 3135, ff. 44–45.

19. *Shenstone's Miscellany*, pp. 8–9; 139–40.

20. British Library Add. Ms. 32,333, f. 77.

21. *Lit. Illus.*, VII, 242, 248.

22. James Grainger, *A Poetical Translation of the Elegies of Tibullus* (London, 1759), p. xiii.

23. *Critical Review*, December, 1758, pp. 476–77.

24. James Grainger, *A Letter to Tobias Smollet, M.D.* (London, 1759).

25. Grainger, *A Poetical Translation*, p. xlii (Ovid's "Elegy on the Death of Tibullus," lines 37–40).

26. *The Works of Samuel Johnson, LL.D.* (London, 1787), III, 240. Lines 53–56 of the translation of Tibullus's First Elegy were taken from Hammond.

27. *The Percy Letters*, vol. 7, *The Correspondence of Thomas Percy & William Shenstone*, ed. Cleanth Brooks (New Haven: Yale University Press, 1977), p. 11. Percy had changed his mind by August, 1758, when he used a different stanza form for an ode "On the Death of Augustus, Earl of Sussex," who had died on January 8, 1758. The ode was not published until 1952 (*Shenstone's Miscellany*, pp. 57–60).

28. Bodleian Ms. Add C. 89, ff. 310–11.

29. *The Library*, May, 1761, pp. 93–95.

30. Ralph Griffiths to Percy, April 23, 1762 (Hyde Collection); Percy to Griffiths, n.d. (Bodleian Ms. Add. C. 89, f. 312). Griffiths informed Percy on April 23 that the article on "Popish Relics" would have been published in the April issue, but the man who was going to write the introduction to it went to the country and left the article in his bureau.

31. Sir James Stonhouse, *Friendly Advice to a Patient: and Spiritual*

Directions for the Uninstructed, 9th ed. (London, 1762), pp. ix–xi;
Scots Magazine, November, 1762, p. 604; *Gentleman's Magazine,*
November, 1762, p. 545.
  32. Bodleian Ms. Percy d.4, ff. 155–57.
  33. British Library Add. Ms. 32,329, ff. 4–8.
  34. Percy's last stanza reads as follows:
        Yes, generous Friend,
        Thy Skill attempts the nobler Part,
        The Will deprav'd to mend,
        To probe and cleanse the ulcerous Heart,
        And, thro' the Saviour's all-restoring Blood,
        To raise to endless Life, the Penitent and Good.

  35. British Library Add. Ms. 32,329, f. 8.
  36. Ibid.

                          Chapter Three

  1. *The Percy Letters,* vol. 5, *The Correspondence of Thomas
Percy & Evan Evans,* ed. Aneirin Lewis (Baton Rouge: Louisiana
State University Press, 1957), p. 82.
  2. The agreements with Dodsley are noted in Percy's Diary
(British Library Add. Ms. 32,336) for March 8, 1759, and March
21–23, 1761. See also *Willis's Current Notes,* 47 (November, 1854),
pp. 90–91. For the agreements with Tonson see *Lit. Illus.,* VI,
556–61 and British Library Add. Ms. 38,728, ff. 167–73.
  3. Harvard, bMS Eng 893 (265), quoted by permission of the
Houghton Library. The letter is quoted in full in Vincent H. Ogburn,
"The Wilkinson MSS. and Percy's Chinese Books," *Review of English
Studies,* 9 (1933): 30.
  4. *The Percy Letters,* vol. 1, *The Correspondence of Thomas
Percy & Edmond Malone,* ed. Arthur Tillotson (Baton Rouge: Lou-
isiana University Press, 1944), p. 192.
  5. Ch'ên Shou-Yi, "Thomas Percy and His Chinese Studies,"
Chinese Social and Political Science Review, 20 (July, 1936), 216.
  6. For the publication date see Ralph Straus, *Robert Dodsley
Poet, Publisher & Playwright* (London: John Lane, 1910), p. 375.
The *Public Advertiser* for November 14, 1761, contains the first
advertisement for the book beginning "This Day was published."
Other dates in the paragraph are taken from Percy's Diary, and
Grainger's letter is in *Lit. Illus.,* VII, 267–70.
  7. T. C. Fan, "Percy's *Hau Kiou Choaan,*" *Review of English
Studies,* 22 (1946), 119.

8. John Francis Davis, *The Fortunate Union, a Romance Translated from the Chinese Original* (London, 1829), I, viii, x.

9. William W. Appleton, *A Cycle of Cathay* (New York: Columbia University Press, 1951), pp. 77, 90.

10. Percy's copy of *Miscellaneous Pieces Related to the Chinese* is in the Bodleian Library (Percy 108, 109).

11. *Public Advertiser*, December 13, 1762.

12. Letter Richard Hurd to Richard Farmer, January 10, 1763, British Library Add. Ms. 32,329, ff. 22–23.

13. Ogburn, "The Wilkinson MSS. and Percy's Chinese Books," 34; letter Grainger to Percy, February, 1758, *Lit. Illus.*, VII, 250.

14. Huntington Library Mss. HM 6173; HM 6511.

15. Ibid., HM 6173, final page, quoted by permission of the Huntington Library.

16. Boswell, *Life of Johnson*, IV, 274.

17. *Gentleman's Magazine*, December, 1784, pp. 891–92. In this list of authors, originally prepared by John Swinton, the *history of the Chinese* is attributed to Swinton himself.

18. *Public Advertiser*, May 28, 1762.

19. Cleanth Brooks, "The Country Parson as Research Scholar: Thomas Percy, 1760–1770," p. 224.

20. The story is contained in a letter of Sir George Etherege to the duke of Buckingham. In making this suggestion I am following the lead of Cleanth Brooks ("The Country Parson as Research Scholar," p. 224).

21. T. C. Fan, "Percy and Du Halde," *Review of English Studies*, 21 (October, 1945), 328–29. Percy's translation of *The Chinese Matron* is also quite different from that in the edition of Du Halde published by John Watts in 1736 (III, 134–55).

22. *Monthly Review*, June, 1762, p. 510.

23. British Library Add. Ms. 32,325, ff. 258, 260.

24. Queen's University of Belfast. Percy's note was written on a card inserted in William Shaw's *Earse Dictionary*, vol. 1.

25. *Percy Letters*, VII, 70, 74.

26. Pages 487–89. It was reprinted in the *Annual Register* for 1761, pp. 236–37.

27. *Percy Letters*, V, 3.

28. Ralph Straus in *Robert Dodsley* gives the date as April 3, but an advertisement in the *Public Advertiser* of April 2 announced publication on that day, and April 3, being a Sunday, would not have been a business day.

29. William Herbert, *Select Icelandic Poetry, Translated from the Originals* (London, 1804), p. 9.

30. Sir Walter Scott, "Herbert's Miscellaneous Poetry," *Edinburgh Review*, October, 1806, pp. 212–13.

31. *Lit. Illus.*, VII, 130.

32. *Percy Letters*, V, 30–31.

33. Margaret Omberg, *Scandinavian Themes in English Poetry, 1760–1800* (Stockholm: Almqvist and Wiksall, 1976), p. 60.

34. Letters Percy to Andrew Millar, December 12, 1762, and John Newbery to Percy, June 9, 1763. Both are in the Hyde Collection.

35. The prose *Edda* "was neither more nor less than a Course of Poetical Lectures drawn up for the use of such young Icelanders as devoted themselves to the profession of *Scald* or POET" (II, xvii). Mallet (and Percy) translated the thirty-three fables of the first part. The more ancient poetic *Edda* is described at the end of the prose *Edda* (II, 201–6).

36. Information from Percy's Diary, July 24 and 26, 1767.

37. *Percy Letters*, V, 116; Diary, February 7, 1767.

38. *Percy Letters*, V, 126.

39. *London Chronicle* and *London Evening-Post*, December 1–3, 1767.

40. *Public Advertiser*, June 8, 1770.

41. *Northern Antiquities*, ed. I. A. Blackwell (London, 1847), pp. 22–45.

42. Northrop Frye, *Fearful Symmetry: A Study of William Blake* (Princeton: Princeton University Press, 1947), pp. 172–73.

43. A fairly full discussion of Percy's *Northern Antiquities* may be found in Omberg, *Scandinavian Themes*, pp. 48–59.

44. *Public Advertiser*, June 13, 1764.

45. *St. James's Magazine*, June, 1764, pp. 322–30; *Critical Review*, July, 1764, pp. 78–79.

46. The close relationship of Percy's translation to the King James version can be seen in parallel passages from 5:15:16. The King James version is as follows:

His legs are as pillars of marble, set upon sockets of fine gold: his countenance is as Lebanon, excellent as the cedars:

His mouth is most sweet: yea, he is altogether lovely. This is my beloved, and this is my friend, O Daughters of Jerusalem.

Percy's version begins differently but ends identically:

His thighs are pillars of marble, fixed upon pedestals of fine gold.

His countenance is like Lebanon: majestic as the cedars.
His mouth is sweetness itself: yea, he is altogether lovely.
This is my beloved, and this is my friend, O daughters of Jerusalem.
(pp. 28–29)

47. *The Song of Solomon Paraphrased* (Edinburgh, 1775), pp. 9, 11, 14.

48. Alexander Ducarel to Percy, April 29, 1782 (British Library Add. Ms. 32,329, ff. 122–23).

49. Diary, August 6, 1764.

50. *The Percy Letters,* vol. 6, *The Correspondence of Thomas Percy & George Paton,* ed. A. F. Falconer (New Haven: Yale University Press, 1961), p. 12.

51. Bodleian Mss. Percy d. 3, d. 4, and d. 5.

52. *Gentleman's Magazine,* July, 1793, p. 662; August, 1793, pp. 683–84. The August account (probably written by Percy's nephew, who was a fellow of St. John's College) asserts that Percy "very properly" took the lead in contrasting "our happy state" with "the misery and horrors exhibited now in France." Percy preached his sermon on July 2 and was awarded the doctor of divinity degree on July 3.

53. Bodleian Ms. Percy d. 5, ff. 60–79.

54. Letter Shute Barrington to Percy, [May 31, 1769], Osborn Collection, Yale University.

55. Joseph Cradock, *Literary and Miscellaneous Memoirs* (London, 1828), I, 241–42. Cradock has Johnson referring to Percy as "Doctor" somewhat prematurely. Percy was awarded the doctorate by Cambridge University the following year.

56. *A Sermon Preached at Christ-Church, Dublin, on the 18th of April, 1790, before ... the Incorporated Society, in Dublin, for Promoting English Protestant Schools, in Ireland* (Dublin, 1790).

57. The dates for 1765 and 1766 are taken from Percy's diary. In 1765, when Percy conducted him on a tour of the Lake District and Scotland, Algernon Percy was only fifteen.

58. Percy was probably the author of a sixteen-line poem signed "T. P." in the *St. James's Chronicle* for April 24–26, 1766: "On a Concert and Ball, for the Benefit and Building of the Middlesex Hospital, and a Ball for the Lying-in Hospital." The duke of Northumberland was president of the Middlesex Hospital. The poem was called to my attention by Betty Rizzo.

59. The pamphlet was reprinted in Nichols's *Literary Illustrations* (VIII, 152–57). References in the text are to that printing.

60. *Percy Letters,* IV, 99–100.

61. Diary, November 30, 1770.

62. Bodleian Ms. Percy c. 6, f. 51. The British Library has a copy of the *Northumberland Houshold Book* without Percy's preface and terminal notes and with a title page dated 1768. I have seen no other copies in this state. It, and perhaps a few other copies, appear to have been used by Percy to elicit comments from his friends before the book was put in final form with his additions.

63. *The Percy Folio Manuscript,* ed. John W. Hales and Frederick J. Furnivall (London, 1868), I, xl.

64, Bodleian Ms. Percy c. 1, f. 123.

65. Alnwick Castle Ms. 93A/29.

66. Bodleian Ms. Percy c. 4, f. 1. The poem was first advertised in the *Public Advertiser,* May 21, 1771.

67. Charles Henry Hartshorne, *Feudal and Military Antiquities* (London, 1858), pp. 221–22.

68. See, for example, John Seymour, *The Companion Guide to the Coast of North-East England* (London: Collins, 1974), p. 74.

69. Hartshorne, p. 212.

70. *Antiquarian Repertory* (London, 1780), III, 41–43; 129–30. In this volume (p. 29) "The Allowance of Cloth . . . to the King's Fool" was also sent in by Percy.

71. Ibid, 130–32; diary, August 24, 1765.

72. Alnwick Castle Ms. 93A/19. Percy submitted the proposed text of the inscription to Horace Walpole, who suggested three changes in a letter dated June 11, 1780. All were incorporated in the inscription.

73. Lord Percy's letters to Percy are in the Boston Public Library (Ms. G.31.39 [1–5]). "The Case of Hugh Baron Percy . . . on His Claim to the Office and Dignity of Lord Great Chamberlain of England" is mentioned in the *Percy Letters,* IV, 145–46 and in Percy's diary for May 9, 10, 11, and 18, 1781. A printed copy of "The Case" is in Alnwick Castle Ms. 93A/20.

74. British Library Add. Ms. 32,329, ff. 101–102.

75. Alnwick Castle Ms. 93A/11.

76. Bodleian Ms. Percy b. 2, f. 1; *Lit. Illus.,* VI, 573.

77. Ibid, VIII, 289. A detailed account of the projected Surrey edition has been published as an appendix to the *Percy Letters,* II, 175–200. The appendix and an earlier, briefer account in *Englische Studien* (February, 1934, pp. 424–30) were written by Cleanth Brooks. An account of the Buckingham edition by M. G. Robinson appears as an appendix to the *Percy Letters,* III, 148–65.

78. Percy's last letter to Steevens (*Lit. Illus.*, VII, 35–36) is dated November 12, 1797.

79. *Lit. Illus.*, VI, 573.

80. *Percy Letters*, II, 197.

81. Ibid, III, 26.

82. Northamptonshire Record Office, box X 1079 E (S) 1211, f. 2.

83. *Percy Letters*, II, 47.

84. Northamptonshire Record Office, box X 1079 E (S) 1211, f. 43.

85. *Lit. Illus.*, VI, 574.

86. Percy correspondence related to these editions is in British Library Add. Ms. 32,329, passim.

87. The *Key to the Rehearsal* is in volume 2 of the 1704 edition of Buckingham's works. Percy's description of it is contained in his "Advertisement" to the *New Key*, which has been printed in the *Percy Letters*, III, 159–61.

88. *Percy Letters*, IV, 1.

89. Northamptonshire Record Office, E (S) 1218.

90. British Library Add. Ms. 35,230, f. 24.

Chapter Four

1. The best discussion of the background of the *Reliques* is contained in Albert B. Friedman's *The Ballad Revival* (Chicago: University of Chicago Press, 1961), to which this chapter is much indebted.

2. Diary, August 19–30, 1761.

3. Henry Bold, *Latine Songs, with Their English: and Poems* (London, 1685), p. 80.

4. Friedman, p. 129. Addison also devoted number 85 of the *Spectator* to a discussion of "The Children in the Wood."

5. *Reliques of Ancient English Poetry* (London, 1765), I, xv.

6. *Percy Letters*, VII, 175–93.

7. Percy's use of the *Collection of Old Ballads* has been carefully analyzed by Stephen Vartin in *Thomas Percy's Reliques: Its Structure and Organization* (Ph.D diss., New York University, 1972).

8. The folio manuscript is British Library Add. Ms. 27,879. It was edited in three volumes by John W. Hales and Frederick J. Furnivall and published as *Bishop Percy's Folio Manuscript* (London, 1867–1868); Percy's flyleaf inscription is printed at I, lxxiv, from which the extract is taken.

9. *Bishop Percy's Folio Manuscript*, I, lxxiv.

10. *Percy Letters*, VII, 3–4.

11. L. F. Powell, "Percy's Reliques," *The Library*, September, 1928, pp. 114–16.

12. *Bishop Percy's Folio Manuscript*, I, xiii.

13. *Percy Letters*, VII, 130, 134.

14. Ibid, p. 119.

15. British Library Add. Ms. 45,867, A28, B40. Percy was granted admission to the Reading Room on April 24, 1761.

16. Like the Shenstone correspondence, all four of these correspondences have been published in separate volumes of *The Percy Letters*.

17. Percy's changes are discussed in Albert B. Friedman, "The First Draft of Percy's *Reliques*," *PMLA*, 69 (December, 1954), 1233–49; and *The Ballad Revival*, pp. 224–25. For discussions of Dalrymple's assistance see the introduction to the *Percy Letters* (vol. 4) and P. G. Thomas, "Bishop Percy and the Scottish Ballad," *TLS*, July 4, 1929, p. 538. David C. Fowler argues persuasively that some of the best-known Scottish ballads ("Sir Patrick Spence" and "Edward, Edward" among them) were revised before they were sent to Percy (*A Literary History of the Popular Ballad* [Durham: Duke University Press, 1968], pp. 239–70).

18. *Percy Letters*, IV, 49.

19. British Library Add. Ms. 32,334, f. 2.

20. Percy's diary entries related to Johnson's visit have been published in Boswell's *Life of Johnson*, I, 553–54.

21. *Percy Letters*, IV, 1.

22. Allen T. Hazen, *Samuel Johnson's Prefaces and Dedications* (New Haven: Yale University Press, 1937), pp. 161–62.

23. Robert Anderson, *The Life of Samuel Johnson, LL.D.*, 3d ed. (Edinburgh, 1815), p. 309.

24. Hazen, pp. 158–68.

25. Diary, November 22, 1764.

26. *Public Advertiser*, February 11, 1765.

27. *Critical Review*, February, 1765, pp. 119–30; *Monthly Review*, April, 1765, pp. 241–53; *Gentleman's Magazine*, April, 1765, pp. 179–83.

28. Diary, March 16, 1765.

29. *Percy Letters*, IV, 94; III, 119.

30. *Four Essays, as Improved and Enlarged in the Second Edition of the Reliques of Ancient English Poetry* (London, 1767). René Wellek said of the essays that they "represent, in many ways, the

best and most learned collection of essays on older English literary history that appeared before Warton" (*The Rise of English Literary History* [Chapel Hill: University of North Carolina Press, 1941], p. 144).

31. The earliest manuscript of *Piers Plowman* is thought to date from about 1372. The attribution to William Langland, whom Percy mistakenly calls Robert, remains uncertain.

32. Wellek, *The Rise of English Literary History*, pp. 154, 158.

33. Boswell, *Life of Johnson*, III, 278.

34. The earliest advertisements I have found for the second edition are those in the *London Chronicle* and *London Evening-Post* for December 1–3, 1767. On June 25, 1767, however, Percy wrote to John Bowle to ask how he could convey a copy of the new edition to him, and on July 13 he wrote to express the hope that "the Books" had reached Bowle in accordance with his directions [University of Cape Town: BC 188, Bowle-Evans Collection, Correspondence between the Reverend Thomas Percy and the Reverend John Bowle, (4) and (5)].

35. Vincent H. Ogburn, "Thomas Percy's Unfinished Collection, Ancient English and Scottish Poems," *ELH*, 3 (1936), 183–89; E. K. A. Mackenzie, "Percy's Great Schemes," *Modern Language Review*, 43 (1948), 34–38.

36. In the first edition "My Mind to Me a Kingdom Is" is at I, 268–71 (11 stanzas). In the second edition it is at I, 292–94 (7 stanzas), and "The Golden Mean" is at I, 303–4 (4 stanzas).

37. Letter Thomas Tyrwhitt to Percy, August 30, 1768, Bodleian Ms. Eng. Lett. d. 59, ff. 17–18.

38. In new footnotes to the Northumberland poems, Percy also writes familiarly of the county and the people. The "shyars thre" in line 14 of "The Ancient Ballad of Chevy-Chase" he identifies in the second edition as the Northumberland districts of Island-shire, Norehamshire, and Bamboroughshire. He notes that "winn their haye" in line 2 of "The Battle of Otterbourne" is "the Northumberland phrase to this day" for "getting in their hay," and two stanzas later he identifies Ottercap Hill, Rodeliffe Cragge, and Green Leyton as "well-known places in Northumberland." In annotating "The More Modern Ballad of Chevy-Chase" he notes that "The Chiviot Hills and circumjacent Wastes are at present void both of Deer and Woods: but formerly they had enough of both to justify the Descriptions attempted here and in the Ancient Ballad" (I, 256).

39. It can be noted that Percy's continuing search permitted him

to add seven items in the second edition to his list of thirty romances supplementary to the essay "On the Ancient Metrical Romances."

40. "Observations on Dr. Percy's Account of Minstrels among the Saxons," *Archaeologia* (London, 1773), II, 100–106.

41. Bodleian Mss. Percy c.11, f.17; Eng. Lett. d. 46, ff. 653–56.

42. *Lit. Illus.*, VIII, 164. The letter was published in *Archaeologia* (London, 1775), III, 310.

43. *The General Biographical Dictionary* (London, 1812–1816), "Joseph Ritson."

44. *A Select Collection of English Songs* (London, 1783), I, lxviii. Thomas Carter's music for Percy's song was printed in the third volume of the collection, pp. 219–20.

45. Bodleian Ms. Percy c. 1, f. 122.

46. Harvard bMS Eng 891 (3), quoted by permission of the Houghton Library. Percy's letter of November 19, 1785, is unsigned and appears to be either a draft or a copy.

47. In his copy (at Yale-Beinecke), Joseph Haslewood tipped in a newspaper announcement of the edition ("This Day is published") marked in pen "July, 1795." This date is consistent with the first discussion of the edition in Percy's correspondence and elsewhere.

48. Percy recalled his nephew's receiving £160 for his part in the fourth edition (Bodleian Ms. Percy c. 3, f. 200).

49. Ibid., f. 59; *Ancient Engleish Metrical Romanceës* (London, 1802), pp. cvii–cviii, n.

50. British Library Add. Ms. 32,335, f. 197.

51. *Lit. Illus.*, VIII, 145; Bertrand H. Bronson, *Joseph Ritson Scholar-at-Arms* (Berkeley: University of California Press, 1938), I, 295.

52. *The Percy Letters*, III, 119; *Willis's Current Notes*, November, 1854, p. 91. In "Percy's Reliques" (p. 136), L. F. Powell cited a June 21, 1774, receipt signed by Percy for twenty guineas paid to him by James Dodsley "for correcting and improving the third edition. . . , which is to consist of a thousand Copies." *Willis's Current Notes*, however, cites a later agreement (March 7, 1775) whereby Dodsley, in consideration of being able to print 1500 copies, relinquished to Percy, as his future property, all the copperplates used in the *Reliques*. Dodsley also agreed to pay Percy forty guineas five years after the presswork on the third edition was completed, and Percy was not to republish the *Reliques* until all 1500 copies were sold.

53. *Bishop Percy's Folio Manuscript*, III, 2.

54. References in the paragraph are to the fourth edition: II, 137; III, 48, 178, 193.

55. *British Critic,* January, 1805, pp. 88–89. Nares had succeeded Percy as vicar of Easton Mauduit.

56. *Lit. Illus.,* VII, 215; Robert Burns, *Select Scotish Songs, Ancient and Modern,* ed. R. H. Cromek (London, 1810), I, 224–30.

Chapter Five

1. Percy's correspondence with the duchess of Northumberland is in British Library Add. Ms. 32,334.

2. In a letter of August 12, 1775, Lord Percy thanked Percy for some twenty letters he had already received (Boston Public Library MS G.3. 39 [6]).

3. *Archaeologia* (London, 1785), VII, 158–59.

4. *Gentleman's Magazine,* March, 1797, pp. 179–80. The article is signed T. P.

5. Ibid., January, 1805, p. 30.

6. Ibid., May, 1802, p. 475; *Lit. Illus.,* VI, 583, n.

7. *Gentleman's Magazine,* May, 1802, pp. 387–91; British Library Add. Ms. 42,516, ff. 129–30.

8. *Lit. Illus.,* VI, 584–85. The poems were published in May, 1803, pp. 454–55.

9. *Lit. Illus.,* VI, 588. The poem was published in January, 1805, p. 64, with notes probably written by Percy.

10. Thomas Romney Robinson, *Juvenile Poems* (Belfast, 1806).

11. By my count, at least. Young Robinson, it should be noted, achieved his subsequent reputation as an astronomer and physicist: he was the inventor of the cup anemometer, among other accomplishments. He died in 1882 at the age of ninety.

12. *Gentleman's Magazine,* March, 1790, p. 191.

13. *British Critic,* September, pp. 286–95; October, pp. 359–65; November, pp. 524–29. The anonymity of the reviewer concealed the fact that Percy was reviewing a book dedicated to himself.

14. Treadway Russell Nash, *The History and Antiquities of Worcestershire* (London, 1781–1799), II, 89–99; John Nichols, *The History and Antiquities of Hinckley* (London, 1782); John Nichols, *The History and Antiquities of the County of Leicester,* vol. 3, pt. 1 (London, 1800). The account of Thurmaston is on pp. 54–60, and p. 66 of the *History . . . of Leicester.*

15. James Boswell, *Boswell for the Defence,* ed. William K. Wimsatt and Frederick A. Pottle (London: Heinemann, 1960), p. 174.

Percy noted in his diary for April 3, 1773, that on that day he purchased the portrait for six guineas. The portrait was by the seventeenth-century artist Isaac Fuller.

16. *Biographia Britannica*, 2d ed. (London, 1784), III, 628–33.

17. Percy's letters to William Cleiveland are in British Library Add. Ms. 32,333. Cleiveland died on October 28, 1794. For an account of the correspondence, see Bertram H. Davis, " 'Dear Cuz': The Letters of Thomas Percy to William Cleiveland," *The New Rambler*, 17 (1976), 11–25.

18. Bodleian Ms. Percy c. 3, ff. 56–77, 156–70.

19. British Library Add. Ms. 32,335, f. 146.

20. Percy also added ten pounds a year to Anna Williams' pension (Robert Anderson, *The Life of Samuel Johnson, LL.D.*, 3d ed. p. 164). The Voltaire-Rolt letters were submitted to the *European Magazine* by Percy and published in the issue for February, 1803.

21. *London Chronicle*, July 3–5, 5–7, 7–10, 1764.

22. Boswell, *Life of Johnson*, IV, 556.

23. The manuscript is in the Hyde Collection.

24. *Critical Review*, October, 1764, pp. 270–77.

25. Boswell, *Life of Johnson*, IV, 556.

26. The attack on Grainger's wife was published in the *Westminster Magazine* for December, 1773 (pp. 685–87) and reprinted in the *Whitehall Evening Post* for January 4–6, 1774. Percy's reply was published in the *Whitehall Evening Post* for January 11–13; parts of it are quoted in Boswell's *Life*, II, 534–35.

27. *The Correspondence and Other Papers of James Boswell Relating to the Making of the Life of Johnson*, ed. Marshall Waingrow (New York: McGraw-Hill, 1969), pp. 393–94, 397–98; C. N. Fifer, "Boswell and the Decorous Bishop," *Journal of English and Germanic Philology*, 61 (January, 1962), 53; Boswell, *Life of Johnson*, IV, 556.

28. *Lit. Illus.*, VII, 71; *European Magazine*, September, 1798, pp. 192–94.

29. *The Works in Verse and Prose of William Shenstone, Esq.* (London, 1764), II, 333–71. The account, Percy wrote, "was begun by Mr. [Richard] Jago, myself and another Friend or two of Mr. Shenstone's . . . in Autumn, 1762 . . . ; but Mr. Shenstone's Death prevented our giving it a more correct finishing" (*Percy Letters*, VII, 216).

30. *Shenstone's Miscellany 1759–1763*, p. xv.

31. *Baldwin's London Weekly Journal*, September 21, 1771; *Johnsonian News Letter*, March, 1977, pp. 9–11. The text of the parody is from *Boswell for the Defence*, pp. 177–78.

32. *Johnsonian Miscellanies*, ed. George Birkbeck Hill (New York, 1897), I, 192.

33. It was finally published by the Oxford University Press in 1932, with a preface by David Nichol Smith.

34. From the translation of "El Marinero de Amor," *Ancient Songs*, p. 49.

35. Shasta M. Bryant, *The Spanish Ballad in English* (Lexington: University Press of Kentucky, 1973), p. 25.

36. *The Yale Edition of the Works of Samuel Johnson*, VIII, 1034. Percy identified the "forked plague" as "cuckold's horns."

37. *Percy Letters*, III, 132.

38. The revised *Works of Shakespeare* was published in 1771. Percy's manuscript glossary is in the Folger Shakespeare Library.

39. Bodleian Ms. Percy c. 1, f. 28.

40. The dispute over Pennant's comments took place on April 12, 1778, and is recorded in Boswell's *Life*, III, 271–78. A fuller and more revealing account is contained in Boswell's journal: *Boswell in Extremes 1776–1778*, ed. Charles McC. Weis and Frederick A. Pottle (London: Heinemann, 1971), pp. 272–75, 302, 309, 310–11, 317–19. For a discussion of Percy's relationships with Johnson, with emphasis on this episode, see Bertram H. Davis, "A Matter for Dispute: Thomas Percy and Samuel Johnson," *Johnson Society Transactions* (1976), 21–39.

41. Joseph Cradock, *Literary and Miscellaneous Memoirs* (London, 1828), I, 206–7.

42. For an account of this dispute, see C. N. Fifer, "Boswell and the Decorous Bishop."

43. Anderson, *The Life of Samuel Johnson, LL.D.*, 3d ed.

44. *The Miscellaneous Works of Oliver Goldsmith, M.D.* (London, 1801). "The Life of Dr. Oliver Goldsmith" is at I, 1–118.

45. *Percy Letters*, I, 17–18, 25–26.

46. A copy of the proposals is at Harvard (*EC75/P4128/ 785p). They have been printed in Katharine C. Balderston, *The History & Sources of Percy's Memoir of Goldsmith* (Cambridge: Cambridge University Press, 1926), pp. 24–25.

47. Thomas Percy's *Life of Dr. Oliver Goldsmith*, ed. Richard L. Harp (Salzburg: University of Salzburg, 1976), p. xviii. In his extensive annotations, Harp has recorded significant parallels and discrepancies between the two texts. Campbell's ms. is in British Library Add. Ms. 42,517.

48. Percy's agreement with Cadell and Davies is dated October 25, 1797 (British Library Add. Ms. 42,516, f. 5). In addition to the

Balderston study and the Harp edition, useful information and comment on Percy's relations with his publishers are contained in T. Shearer and A. Tillotson, "Percy's Relations with Cadell and Davies," *The Library,* 15 (September, 1934), 224–36, and in Theodore Besterman, *The Publishing Firm of Cadell and Davies* (Oxford: Oxford University Press, 1938), pp. xxii–xxvii.

- 49. Percy's statement is printed in Shearer and Tillotson, pp. 227–29.

50. Samuel Glover, *Life of Dr. Oliver Goldsmith* (London, 1774).

51. *The Collected Letters of Oliver Goldsmith,* ed. Katharine C. Balderston (Cambridge: Cambridge University Press, 1928).

Chapter Six

1. The numbers, of course, are only of those letters that I have become aware of in the course of this study. There may be many more. I have been unable to trace, for example, a good many letters which were auctioned during the 1884 Sotheby sale of Percy's manuscripts.

2. Some of Percy's letters to Paton had been published in 1830 (*Letters . . . To George Paton,* ed. James Maidment [Edinburgh, 1830]), and much of the Percy-Shenstone correspondence had been published in 1909 (*Thomas Percy und William Shenstone,* ed. Hans Hecht [Strassburg, 1909]).

3. Joseph Cradock, *Literary and Miscellaneous Memoirs,* I, 243.

4. *Letters of Eminent Persons Addressed to David Hume* (London, 1849), pp. 317–22; *History of England* (London, 1773), III, 461. Hume did not appreciably alter his view, but he did delete the word "niggardly": *History of England* (London, 1778), III, 461.

5. Many additional letters in these two correspondences, most of them written by Percy, remain untraced.

6. Percy's letters to his wife are in British Library Add. Ms. 32,335.

7. *Percy Letters,* III, 131–32.

8. Bertrand H. Bronson, "A Sense of the Past: The Percy Correspondence," in *Facets of the Enlightenment* (Berkeley: University of California Press, 1968), p. 185.

9. British Library Add. Ms. 32,335, ff. 169–70. Percy's letters to Thomas Apperley are divided among a number of public and private collections.

10. *Percy Letters,* II, 200.

11. The *Gentleman's Magazine* articles are in the issues for August,

1793; April, June, July, October, and December, 1794; January, February, July, August, and September, 1795.

12. E. H. W. Meyerstein, *A Life of Thomas Chatterton* (New York: Scribners, 1930), pp. 56, 211.

13. Margaret Forbes, *Beattie and His Friends* (Westminster: Constable, 1904), p. 56.

14. Margaret R. Lowery, *Windows of the Morning* (New Haven: Yale University Press, 1940), passim; G. E. Bentley, Jr., "Blake and Percy's *Reliques*," *Notes and Queries* 201 (August, 1956), 352–53. Blake's copy of the *Reliques* is in the library of Wellesley College.

15. *The Letters of Sir Walter Scott,* ed. Sir Herbert Grierson (London: Constable, 1932), I, 108.

16. Essay supplementary to the preface to the second edition of the *Lyrical Ballads, The Poetical Works of William Wordsworth*. ed. Thomas Hutchinson (London: Oxford University Press, 1895), p. 949.

17. John L. Mahoney, "Some Antiquarian and Literary Influences of Percy's *Reliques*," *College Language Association Journal*, 7 (1964), 242.

18. John Livingston Lowes, *The Road to Xanadu* (Boston: Houghton Mifflin, 1927), pp. 244, 249, 331, 332, 336, 338n.

19. Stephen Maxfield Parrish, *The Art of the Lyrical Ballads* (Cambridge: Harvard University Press, 1973), p. 226. Parrish also discusses Wordsworth's adaptation of "Lady Bothwell's Lament" (pp. 121–23).

20. *Wordsworth and Coleridge Lyrical Ballads 1798*, ed. H. Littledale (London: Oxford University Press, 1924), p. 144.

21. Donald Revel Tuttle, "*Christabel* Sources in Percy's *Reliques* and the Gothic Romances," *PMLA*, 53 (June, 1938), 445–74

22. *Critical Review*, February, 1765, p. 123.

23. Elsie I. M. Boyd, "The Influence of Percy's 'Reliques of Ancient English Poetry' on German Literature," *Modern Language Quarterly*, 7 (October, 1904), 80–99.

24. Actually there were more than four since it was pirated in Dublin in 1766 and published at least twice in Germany before 1811.

Selected Bibliography

PRIMARY SOURCES

There is no collected edition of Percy's works. Included below are separately published works of Percy's lifetime and significant new works published since his death.

Hau Kiou Choaan or The Pleasing History. 4 vols. London: R. and J. Dodsley, 1761.

The Matrons. London: R. and J. Dodsley, 1762.

Miscellaneous Pieces Relating to the Chinese. 2 vols. London: R. and J. Dodsley, 1762.

Five Pieces of Runic Poetry. London: R. and J. Dodsley, 1763.

The Song of Solomon. London: R. and J. Dodsley, 1764.

Reliques of Ancient English Poetry. 3 vols. London: J. Dodsley, 1765.

―――――. 2d ed. 3 vols. London: J. Dodsley, 1767.

―――――. 3d ed. 3 vols. London: J. Dodsley, 1775.

―――――. 4th ed. 3 vols. London: F. and C. Rivington, 1794 [1795].

―――――. Edited by Henry B. Wheatley. 3 vols. London: 1886; reprint ed., New York: Dover, 1966.

Four Essays, as Improved and Enlarged in the Second Edition of the Reliques of Ancient English Poetry. London: J. Dodsley, 1767.

A Letter Describing the Ride to Hulne Abbey from Alnwick in Northumberland. Privately printed, [1765].

A Key to the New Testament. London: L. Davis and C. Reymers, 1766.

―――――. 2d ed. London: Lockyer Davis, 1773.

―――――. 3d ed. London: Lockyer Davis, 1779.

―――――. 4th ed. London: F. and C. Rivington and W. Richardson, 1792.

Northern Antiquities. 2 vols. London: T. Carnan, 1770.

A Sermon Preached before the Sons of the Clergy, at Their Anniversary Meeting, in the Cathedral Church of St. Paul, on Thursday, May 11, 1769. London: John and Francis Rivington, [1770].

The Regulations and Establishment of the Houshold of Henry Algernon Percy. London: privately printed, 1770.

The Hermit of Warkworth. London: T. Davies and S. Leacroft, 1771.

"Percy, Duke of Northumberland." In *The Peerage of England.* London, 1779. II, 280–490.

A Sermon Preached at Christ-Church, Dublin, on the 18th of April, before . . . the Incorporated Society, in Dublin, for Promoting English Protestant Schools, in Ireland. Dublin: The Incorporated Society, 1790.

"The Life of Dr. Oliver Goldsmith." In *The Miscellaneous Works of Oliver Goldsmith, M.D.* Vol. 1. London: J. Johnson, 1801.

Illustrations of the Literary History of the Eighteenth Century. Edited by John Nichols and John Bowyer Nichols. London: Nichols, 1817–1858; reprint ed., New York: Kraus, 1966. Vols. 6–8.

Ancient Songs Chiefly on Moorish Subjects. Oxford: Oxford University Press, 1932.

The Percy Letters. General Editors. David Nichol Smith and Cleanth Brooks, later Cleanth Brooks and A. F. Falconer. Vols. 1–5. Baton Rouge: Louisiana State University Press. Vols. 6–7. New Haven: Yale University Press. Vol. 1, *The Correspondence of Thomas Percy & Edmond Malone,* edited by Arthur Tillotson (1944; reprinted with additions [Yale University Press, 1960]); vol. 2, *The Correspondence of Thomas Percy & Richard Farmer.* edited by Cleanth Brooks (1946); vol. 3, *The Correspondence of Thomas Percy & Thomas Warton,* edited by M. G. Robinson and Leah Dennis (1951); vol. 4, *The Correspondence of Thomas Percy & David Dalrymple, Lord Hailes,* edited by A. F. Falconer (1954); vol. 5, *The Correspondence of Thomas Percy & Evan Evans,* edited by Aneirin Lewis (1957); vol. 6, *The Correspondence of Thomas Percy & George Paton,* edited by A. F. Falconer (1961); vol. 7, *The Correspondence of Thomas Percy & William Shenstone,* edited by Cleanth Brooks (1977).

Shenstone's Miscellany. Edited by Ian A. Gordon. Oxford: Clarendon Press, 1952.

SECONDARY SOURCES

1. Books

APPLETON, WILLIAM W. *A Cycle of Cathay: The Chinese Vogue in England during the Seventeenth and Eighteenth Centuries.* New York: Columbia University Press, 1951. A readable and informative account of the extraordinary English interest in China during this period, with considerable attention to Percy's Chinese works.

BALDERSTON, KATHARINE C. *The History & Sources of Percy's Memoir*

of Goldsmith. Cambridge: Cambridge University Press, 1926;
reprint ed., New York: Kraus, 1969. Of particular interest for
its analysis, not always favorable to Percy, of Percy's relationships with his publishers.

Bishop Percy's Folio Manuscript. Edited by John W. Hales and Fred-
erick J. Furnivall. 3 vols. London: Trübner, 1867–1868. Vol. 4.
Loose and Humorous Songs. Edited by Frederick J. Furnivall.
London: The editor, 1868; reprint ed., Detroit: Singing Tree
Press, 1968. The only printing of the entire manuscript, by
editors severely critical of Percy's editorial practice.

BOSWELL, JAMES. *Boswell's Life of Johnson.* Edited by George Birkbeck Hill; revised and enlarged by L. F. Powell. 6 vols. Oxford:
Clarendon Press, 1934–1950. Contains a variety of information
supplied by Percy and about him.

————. *Boswell in Extremes 1776–1778.* Edited by Charles McC.
Weis and Frederick A. Pottle. London: Heinemann, 1971. Gives
a fuller account than the *Life* of the Johnson-Percy dispute over
Pennant's comments on Alnwick Castle.

————. *The Correspondence and Other Papers of James Boswell
Relating to the Making of the Life of Johnson.* Edited by Marshall
Waingrow. New York: McGraw-Hill, 1969. The best source of
information on Percy's dispute with Boswell about some of the
materials in the *Life.*

BRONSON, BERTRAND H. *Joseph Ritson Scholar-at-Arms.* 2 vols. Berkeley: University of California Press, 1938. An exhaustive study
which recounts the Ritson-Percy controversy from Ritson's point
of view.

————. *The Traditional Tunes of the Child Ballads.* 4 vols. Princeton: Princeton University Press, 1959–1972. A comprehensive
and monumental collection, with transcriptions and discussions
of the music of some 300 ballads (plus variants), including many
in the Percy folio manuscript.

BRYANT, SHASTA M. *The Spanish Ballad in English.* Studies in Romance Languages no. 8. Lexington: University Press of Kentucky,
1973. Sets Percy's ballad translations in context.

CARVER, J. D. "Thomas Percy and the Making of the *Reliques of
Ancient English Poetry.*" B.Litt. thesis, Oxford University, 1973.
Some useful background information and analyses.

CHILD, FRANCIS J. *English and Scottish Popular Ballads.* 5 vols.
Boston: Houghton Mifflin; London: Sterns, Son, and Stiles,
1882–1898; reprint ed., New York: Cooper Square, 1965. The
comprehensive collection of popular ballads and their variants.

CHURCHILL, IRVING L. "The Early Literary Career of Thomas Percy." Ph.D diss., Yale University, 1932. Contains extensive information on Percy's work up to and including the *Reliques*.

CRADOCK, JOSEPH. *Literary and Miscellaneous Memoirs*. 4 vols. London: Nichols, 1828; reprint ed., Franborough: Gregg International, 1972. Considerable but not always reliable information about Percy's relations with Johnson and other matters.

DAVIS, JOHN FRANCIS, trans. *The Fortunate Union, a Romance*. 2 vols. London: Murray, 1829. A translation of *Hau Kiou Choaan*, with informative comments on Percy's translation.

FOWLER, DAVID C. *A Literary History of the Popular Ballad*. Durham: Duke University Press, 1968. A penetrating study, with extensive chapters on both the folio manuscript and the *Reliques*.

FRIEDMAN, ALBERT B. *The Ballad Revival: Studies in the Influence of Popular on Sophisticated Poetry*. Chicago: University of Chicago Press, 1961. An indispensable history and analysis.

FRYE, NORTHROP. *Fearful Symmetry: A Study of William Blake*. Princeton: Princeton University Press, 1947. Cites Blake's indebtedness to Percy's Nordic studies.

GAUSSEN, ALICE C. C. *Percy: Prelate and Poet*. London: Smith, Elder, 1908. The only full-length biography. Outdated, but based on numerous unpublished materials and still useful.

GEROULD, GORDON HALL. *The Ballad of Tradition*. Oxford: Clarendon Press, 1932. Not very helpful with Percy, but contains useful general information on the ballad.

HARP, RICHARD L., ed. *Thomas Percy's Life of Dr. Oliver Goldsmith*. Salzburg Studies in English Literature. Salzburg: Institut für Englische Sprache und Literatur, University of Salzburg, 1976. Contains a highly informative introduction and notes.

HARTSHORNE, CHARLES HENRY, *Memoirs Illustrative of the History and Antiquities of Northumberland*. Vol. 2. *Feudal and Military Antiquities of Northumberland and the Scottish Borders*. London: Bell and Daldy, 1858. One chapter is devoted to the Warkworth hermitage and Percy's poem.

HAZEN, ALLEN T., ed. *Samuel Johnson's Prefaces and Dedications*. New Haven: Yale University Press, 1937. Provides bibliographical information about the *Reliques* and reprints the dedication.

JOHNSTON, ARTHUR. *Enchanted Ground: The Study of the Medieval Romance in the Eighteenth Century*. London: Athlone Press, 1964. Assesses Percy's work with the ancient English romances.

LAWS, G. MALCOLM, JR. *The British Literary Ballad: A Study in*

Imitation. Carbondale: Southern Illinois University Press, 1972. A study of the ballad as an art form.

LOWERY, MARGARET R. *Windows of the Morning*. New Haven: Yale University Press, 1940. Discusses William Blake's use of the *Reliques*.

OGBURN, VINCENT H. "New Light on the Life and Works of Bishop Thomas Percy." Ph.D. diss., Stanford University, 1935. Includes a variety of interesting material and commentary, much of it published in articles listed in part 2 of this bibliography.

OMBERG, MARGARET. *Scandinavian Themes in English Poetry 1760–1800*. Stockholm: Almqvist and Wiksall, 1976. Percy's contributions through his translations of Mallet and runic poetry are judiciously reviewed.

REIBERG, RUFUS. "The Later Literary Career of Thomas Percy: 1766–1811." Ph.D. diss., Yale University, 1952. Does for the later career what Churchill did for the early career.

SNYDER, E. D. *The Celtic Revival in English Literature*. Cambridge: Harvard University Press, 1923. Lauds Percy for his pioneering work.

STRAUS, RALPH. *Robert Dodsley: Poet, Publisher & Playwright*. London: John Lane, 1910. A biography of Percy's major publisher, with information on some early Percy editions.

VARTIN, STEPHEN. "Thomas Percy's *Reliques*: Its Structure and Organization." Ph.D. diss., New York University, 1972. A perceptive study of the *Reliques* and of its indebtedness to earlier collections.

WELLEK, RENÉ. *The Rise of English Literary History*. Chapel Hill: University of North Carolina Press, 1941. Assesses Percy's pioneering work in literary history.

2. Articles

BAINE, RODNEY M. "Percy's Own Copies of the *Reliques*." *Harvard Library Bulletin*, 5 (1951), 273–77. The prepublication copies of the first edition provide a number of insights into the text.

BATE, WALTER JACKSON. "Percy's Use of His Folio-Manuscript." *Journal of English and Germanic Philology*, 43 (1944), 337–48. An incisive examination of Percy's editorial practice.

BOYD, ELSIE I. M. "The Influence of Percy's "Reliques of Ancient English Poetry' on German Literature." *Modern Language Quarterly*, 7 (1904), 80–99. The stimulus given by the *Reliques* to Bürger, Herder, and numerous others.

BRONSON, BERTRAND H. "A Sense of the Past." *Sewanee Review*, 67

(1959), 145–55; reprinted in Bronson, *Facets of the Enlightenment* (Berkeley: University of California Press, 1968), pp. 173–86. A review of *The Percy Letters.*

BROOKS, CLEANTH. "The Country Parson as Research Scholar: Thomas Percy, 1760–1770." *Papers of the Bibliographical Society of America,* 53 (1959), 219–39. An account of Percy's miraculous years.

CHURCHILL, IRVING L. "Thomas Percy, Scholar." In *The Age of Johnson Essays Presented to Chauncey Brewster Tinker.* New Haven: Yale University Press, 1949. Pp. 91–97. Commends Percy's scholarly practice in works other than the *Reliques.*

DAVIS, BERTRAM H. " 'Dear Cuz': The Letters of Thomas Percy to William Cleiveland." *New Rambler,* 17 (1976), 11–25. A discussion of Percy's unpublished correspondence with a favorite cousin.

————. "A Matter for Dispute: Thomas Percy and Samuel Johnson." *Johnson Society Transactions* (1976), 21–39. The relations of Percy and Johnson, with special attention to the dispute over Pennant's remarks about Alnwick Castle.

DENNIS, LEAH. "Thomas Percy: Antiquarian *vs.* Man of Taste." *PMLA,* 57 (1942), 140–54. Left to himself, Percy would have printed literal texts of the *Reliques's* poems; as a result of Shenstone's influence he turned from the literal toward a joint appeal to the antiquarian and the man of taste.

FAN, TSEN CHUNG. "Percy and Du Halde." *Review of English Studies,* 21 (1945), 326–29. Sources of Percy's Chinese works.

————. "Percy's *Hau Kiou Choaan.*" *Review of English Studies,* 22 (1946), 117–25. An analysis of Percy's translation and editorial work.

FIFER, C. N. "Boswell and the Decorous Bishop." *Journal of English and Germanic Philology,* 61 (1962), 48–56. An unflattering view of Percy in his relations with Boswell.

FRIEDMAN, ALBERT B. "The First Draft of Percy's *Reliques.*" *PMLA,* 69 (1954), 1233–49. An interesting glimpse into an early stage of the *Reliques.*

————. "Percy's Folio Manuscript Revalued." *Journal of English and Germanic Philology,* 53 (1954), 524–31. Percy's use of his manuscript was more extensive than Furnivall's comment (that he used only 45 of 191 titles) suggests.

KITTREDGE, GEORGE LYMAN. "Percy and His Nancy." In *Manly Anniversary Studies in Language and Literature.* Chicago: University of Chicago Press, 1923. Pp. 204–18. The English and Scottish versions of Percy's best known poem, along with some later imitations.

KORSHIN, PAUL J. "Robert Anderson's *Life of Johnson* and Early Interpretive Biography." *Huntington Library Quarterly,* 36 (1973), 239–53. Discusses Percy's contributions to Anderson's *Life of Johnson.*

MACKENZIE, EILEEN. "Thomas Percy and Ballad Correctness." *Review of English Studies,* 21 (1945), 58–60. Percy's aim in completing the fragmentary ballads was to adapt them to eighteenth-century ideas of poetic correctness.

MACKENZIE, E. K. A. "Thomas Percy's Great Schemes." *Modern Language Review,* 43 (1948), 34–38. Cites some of Percy's numerous projects either left incomplete or never really begun.

MACKENZIE, M. L. "The Great Ballad Collectors: Percy, Herd, Ritson." *Studies in Scottish Literature,* 2 (1965), 213–33. A comparison of editorial methods, with a clear preference for Herd's and Ritson's.

MAHONEY, JOHN L. "Some Antiquarian and Literary Influences of Percy's *Reliques.*" *College Language Association Journal,* 7 (1964), 240–46. Influences on Coleridge, Scott, and Wordsworth.

MASON, J. F. A. "Bishop Percy's Account of His Own Education." *Notes and Queries,* 204 (1959), 404–8. Information about Percy's early life primarily from British Library Add. Ms. 32,326.

MILLAR, BRANFORD P. "Eighteenth-Century Views of the Ballad." *Western Folklore,* 9 (1950), 124–35. Discusses ballad classification, the selling of single ballads, and contemporary prints suggesting ballad popularity and uses.

MILNER-BARRY, ALDA. "A Note on the Early Literary Relations of Oliver Goldsmith and Thomas Percy." *Review of English Studies,* 2 (1926), 51–61. On Percy's friendship with Goldsmith, particularly as it relates to Percy's Chinese works.

MOORE, ARTHUR K. "*The Literary Status of the English Popular Ballad.*" *Comparative Literature,* 10 (1958), 1–20. Child's restrictive classification of popular ballads has created false impressions of ballad uniformity.

OGBURN, VINCENT H. "A Forgotten Chapter in the Life of Percy." *Review of English Studies,* 12 (1936), 202–8. Some of Percy's Dromore activities.

———. "Further Notes on Thomas Percy." *PMLA,* 51 (1936), 449–58. On Percy's connections with Lady Longueville and the Northumberland family.

———. "The Wilkinson MSS. and Percy's Chinese Books." *Review of English Studies,* 9 (1933), 30–36. Percy's use of the Chinese manuscripts borrowed from Captain Wilkinson.

POWELL, L. F. "Hau Kiou Choaan." *Review of English Studies,* 2 (1926), 446–55. Reviews the publication history.

————. "Percy's Reliques." *The Library,* 9 (1928), 113–37. The publication history of the *Reliques,* with a discussion of the cancels.

RANDALL, DAVID A. "Percy's *Reliques* and Its Cancel Leaves." *New Colophon,* 1 (1948), 404–7. Supplements Powell and Hazen from a copy of the *Reliques* containing some of the cancels.

SHEARER, THOMAS, and TILLOTSON, ARTHUR. "Percy's Relations with Cadell and Davies." *The Library,* 15 (1934), 224–36. Finds Percy much less at fault than the publishers of his life of Goldsmith.

THOMAS, P. G. "Bishop Percy and the Scottish Ballads." *TLS,* July 4, 1929, p. 538. Details some of Percy's literary indebtedness, particularly to David Dalrymple.

TUTTLE, DONALD R. "*Christabel* Sources in Percy's *Reliques* and the Gothic Romances." *PMLA,* 53 (1938), 445–74. *Christabel* contains traces of three *Reliques* ballads.

URE, PETER. "The Widow of Ephesus: Some Reflections on an International Comic Theme." *Durham University Journal,* 49 (1956), 1–9. Finds Percy's adaptation for *The Matrons* the furthest removed from the brutality of the medieval versions of Petronius's tale.

WATKIN-JONES, A. "Bishop Percy and the Scottish Ballads." *Essays and Studies by Members of the English Association,* 18 (1933), 110–21. Percy's association with the Scottish antiquarians, particularly Dalrymple and Paton.

————. "A Pioneer Hispanist: Thomas Percy." *Bulletin of Spanish Studies,* 14 (1937), 3–9. On Percy's translations of Spanish poetry and his projected edition of *Don Quixote.*

Willis's Current Notes, no. 47 (November, 1854), 90–91. Untitled article. Information on publication dates and payments to Percy for some of his early works, based on Dodsley records.

WORDSWORTH, WILLIAM. "Essay, Supplementary to the Preface to the Second Edition of *Lyrical Ballads.*" In *The Poetical Works of Wordsworth.* Edited by Thomas Hutchinson. London: Oxford University Press, 1928. Pp. 944–53.

3. Auction Catalogs

Catalogue of Manuscript Ballads, Songs and other Poems; Autograph

Letters and Manuscripts; MS. Pedigrees of the Percy and other Families connected with the Earls & Dukes of Northumberland; Valuable Printed Songs and Ballads, with MS. Notes and Glossarial Annotations. By the Right Reverend Thomas Percy. London: Sotheby, Wilkinson & Hodge, April 29, 1884.

The Library of Thomas Percy. London: Sotheby & Co., June 23, 1969.

Index

"Adam Bell, Clym of the Clough, and William of Cloudesley," 82
Addison, Joseph, 69, 71, 72, 73, 74, 91, 131. *See also The Guardian; The Spectator; The Tatler*
Advocates' Library, 127
Aiken, John, 27
"Alcanzor and Zayda," 76
Alfred, King of England, 93, 94, 95
Alliterative verse, 85, 86
Alnmouth (Northumberland), 59
Alnwick (Northumberland), 20, 22, 57, 59, 65, 66, 79, 119
Anderson, Robert, 15, 22, 48, 107, 116, 125, 126, 133-34; *The Life of Samuel Johnson, LL.D.*, 120-21
Anlaff, King of Denmark, 93, 94
Antiquarian Repertory, The, 62, 65, 133
Apperley, Thomas, 128
Appleton, William, 41
Archaeologia, 96, 111, 133
"Aspiring Shepherd, The," 91
Astley Abbots (Shropshire), 17, 24, 75, 141
Attiret, Jean-Denis, 42
"Auld Good Man, The," 90
Ayloffe, Sir Joseph, 93

"Baffled Knight, The," 138
Baildon, Joseph, 27
Balderston, Katharine, 123
"Barbara Allen's Cruelty," 89
Barrett, Stephen, 30
Bath (Somersetshire), 23, 26, 27, 75
Battle of Ballynahinch, The, 111

"Battle of Otterbourne, The," 79, 81, 88, 91, 92, 135
Beattie, James: *The Minstrel*, 133
"Beggar's Daughter of Bednall-Green, The," 99, 105, 138
Belfast, 111
Bentley, G. E., 133
Binnel, Robert, 31, 53, 75
Biographia Britannica, 114
Biographia Dramatica, 115
Birch, Thomas, 70
Bishop Percy's Folio Manuscript, 62, 105, 130
Blackwell, I. A., 52
Blakeway, Edward, 57, 78
Blake, William, 52, 138; "Mad Song," 133
Blount, Thomas, 76
Bold, Henry: *Latine Songs*, 73
"Bonny Earl of Murray, The," 89
Bossuet, Jacques-Benigne, 54
Boswell, James, 20, 113-14, 119-20, 126; *Boswell's Life of Johnson*, 79, 115, 116, 121, 123
Bowle, John, 151n38
"Boy and the Mantle, The," 82, 88
Boyd, Elsie, I. M., 137-38
Boyd, Henry, 68, 122
Boy's Percy, The, 139
Brentford (Middlesex), 59
"Bride's Burial, The," 91
Bridgnorth (Shropshire), 16-17, 57, 141n7
British Critic, The, 107, 112, 113
British Museum, 72, 78
Bronson, Bertrand, 128
Brooke, Charlotte: *Reliques of Ancient Irish Poetry*, 132

167